Self-Injury

Self-Injury

Your Questions Answered

Romeo Vitelli

Q&A Health Guides

GREENWOOD™

An Imprint of ABC-CLIO, LLC

Santa Barbara, California • Denver, Colorado

Library of Congress Cataloging-in-Publication Data

Names: Vitelli, Romeo, author.
Title: Self-injury : your questions answered / Romeo Vitelli.
Description: Santa Barbara, California : Greenwood, an imprint of ABC-CLIO, LLC, [2018] | Series: Q&A health guides | Includes bibliographical references and index.
Identifiers: LCCN 2017036172 (print) | LCCN 2017051014 (ebook) | ISBN 9781440854453 (ebook) | ISBN 9781440854446 (alk. paper)
Subjects: LCSH: Self-mutilation—Diagnosis—Popular works. | Self-mutilation—Treatment—Popular works. | Self-mutilation—Prevention—Popular works.
Classification: LCC RC552.S4 (ebook) | LCC RC552.S4 V58 2018 (print) | DDC 616.85/82—dc23
LC record available at https://lccn.loc.gov/2017036172

ISBN: 978-1-4408-5444-6 (print)
        978-1-4408-5445-3 (ebook)

22   21   20   19   18   1   2   3   4   5

This book is also available as an eBook.

Greenwood
An Imprint of ABC-CLIO, LLC

ABC-CLIO, LLC
130 Cremona Drive, P.O. Box 1911
Santa Barbara, California 93116-1911
www.abc-clio.com

This book is printed on acid-free paper ∞

Manufactured in the United States of America

This book is dedicated to my two sisters, Sue and Nancy, for their support. It is also dedicated to all of my self-harming clients, both in the prison system and living in the community, and I thank you for the insight you provided. May this book help others find a way to move past their self-harming and really live their lives.

Contents

Series Foreword

All of us have questions about our health. Is this normal? Should I be doing something differently? Whom should I talk to about my concerns? And our modern world is full of answers. Thanks to the Internet, there's a wealth of information at our fingertips, from forums where people can share their personal experiences to Wikipedia articles to the full text of medical studies. But finding the right information can be an intimidating and difficult task—some sources are written at too high a level, others have been oversimplified, while still others are heavily biased or simply inaccurate.

Q&A Health Guides address the needs of readers who want accurate, concise answers to their health questions, authored by reputable and objective experts, and written in clear and easy-to-understand language. This series focuses on the topics that matter most to young adult readers, including various aspects of physical and emotional well-being as well as other components of a healthy lifestyle. These guides will also serve as a valuable tool for parents, school counselors, and others who may need to answer teens' health questions.

All books in the series follow the same format to make finding information quick and easy. Each volume begins with an essay on health literacy and why it is so important when it comes to gathering and evaluating health information. Next, the top five myths and misconceptions that surround the topic are dispelled. The heart of each guide is a collection of questions and answers, organized thematically. A selection of five case studies provides real-world examples to illuminate key concepts. Rounding out each volume are a directory of resources, glossary, and index.

It is our hope that the books in this series will not only provide valuable information but will also help guide readers toward a lifetime of healthy decision making.

Acknowledgments

I would like to thank the various researchers and therapists whose efforts helped make this book possible. Thanks also go to Maxine Taylor of ABC-CLIO and their excellent support staff as well as those colleagues of mine who were kind enough to review sections of this book and provide helpful suggestions on how it could be improved.

Introduction

My body is a journal in a way. It's like what sailors used to do, where every tattoo meant something, a specific time in your life when you make a mark on yourself, whether you do it yourself with a knife or with a professional tattoo artist.
—Johnny Depp

In talking about the series of scars still visible along one of his arms, actor Johnny Depp remains candid about the self-cutting that was once part of his life. And the cutting didn't just take place during the dark times. "Good times, bad times, it didn't matter. There was no ceremony. It wasn't like 'Okay, this just happened, I have to go hack a piece of my flesh off.'" Depp along with other celebrities such as Angelina Jolie, Megan Fox, Amy Winehouse, and Drew Barrymore are coming forward with their stories of overcoming self-harm like never before.

But this is just the tip of the iceberg in many ways. Because most people who engage in nonsuicidal self-injury (self-harm for short) prefer to stay hidden, we will likely never know how common it really is or how much of a health problem it has become in recent years. But there certainly has been a renaissance of interest in self-harm these past few years with online communities, telephone support lines, websites, and support organizations in countries around the world (many of which are included in the Directory of Resources). Despite this renewed interest, it is more important than ever that self-harmers be provided with accurate information so that they can get the help they need.

Though self-harm can occur at any age, most self-harmers tend to be adolescents and young adults, with surveys suggesting as many as 12–24 percent having harmed themselves at some point and 6–8 percent or more reporting chronic self-injuring that can last well into adulthood. And self-harming behavior can be found in every culture and in every period of our history.

Though most self-harm attempts involve cutting, the sheer range of different ways people can engage in self-harm can be mind-boggling. While treatment is usually available, the shame and guilt surrounding self-harm often mean that people harming themselves are unlikely to seek help or even medical treatment for their self-harm attempts—at least until the injuries become too severe to hide.

With the growing awareness of how common self-harm really is, health organizations around the world are mobilizing to provide better treatment options for self-harmers and their families. Unfortunately, the misconceptions about self-harming, often spread by well-meaning friends and family members, as well as through the Internet, can add to the burden many self-harmers face.

Self-Injury: Your Questions Answered debunks some of the misconceptions about self-harm and discusses how damaging these widely held beliefs can be. The book answers many of the most common questions people are likely to ask about self-harm and is broken down into different sections to help readers focus on what is most important to them. Sections include General Information; Causes and Risk Factors; Culture, Media, and Self-Injury; as well as Assessment, Treatment, Prevention, and Life after Self-Injury. Along with case studies exploring different aspects of self-harm, a Directory of Resources is also provided for people seeking additional information.

This book is intended to provide basic information to anyone whose life has been affected by self-harm, whether they are the self-harmers themselves, concerned friends, family members, teachers, or treatment professionals. Though it is written in commonsense language for anyone to understand, a glossary is also provided for any technical terms you may not recognize.

For self-harmers and family members, the most critical thing to remember is that the right help is out there; you just need to be willing to find it. Good luck!

Guide to Health Literacy

On her 13th birthday, Samantha was diagnosed with type 2 diabetes. She consulted her mom and her aunt, both of whom also have type 2 diabetes, and decided to go with their strategy of managing diabetes by taking insulin. As a result of participating in an after-school program at her middle school that focused on health literacy, she learned that she can help manage the level of glucose in her bloodstream by counting her carbohydrate intake, following a diabetic diet, and exercising regularly. But, what exactly should she do? How does she keep track of her carbohydrate intake? What is a diabetic diet? How long should she exercise and what type of exercise should she do? Samantha is a visual learner, so she turned to her favorite source of media, YouTube, to answer these questions. She found videos from individuals around the world sharing their experiences and tips, doctors (or at least people who have "Dr." in their YouTube channel names), government agencies such as the National Institutes of Health, and even video clips from cat lovers who have cats with diabetes. With guidance from the librarian and the health and science teachers at her school, she assessed the credibility of the information in these videos and even compared their suggestions to some of the print resources that she was able to find at her school library. Now, she knows exactly how to count her carbohydrate level, how to prepare and follow a diabetic diet, and how much (and what) exercise is needed daily. She intends to share her findings with her mom and her aunt, and now she wants to create a chart that summarizes what she has learned that she can share with her doctor.

Samantha's experience is not unique. She represents a shift in our society; an individual no longer views himself or herself as a passive recipient of medical care but as an active mediator of his or her own health. However, in this era when any individual can post his or her opinions and experiences with a particular health condition online with just a few clicks or publish a memoir, it is vital that people know how to assess the credibility of health information. Gone are the days when "publishing" health information required intense vetting. The health information landscape is highly saturated, and people have innumerable sources where they can find information about practically any health topic. The sources (whether print, online, or a person) that an individual consults for health information are crucial because the accuracy and trustworthiness of the information can potentially affect his or her overall health. The ability to find, select, assess, and use health information constitutes a type of literacy—health literacy—that everyone must possess.

THE DEFINITION AND PHASES OF HEALTH LITERACY

One of the most popular definitions for health literacy comes from Ratzan and Parker (2000), who describe health literacy as "the degree to which individuals have the capacity to obtain, process, and understand basic health information and services needed to make appropriate health decisions." Recent research has extrapolated health literacy into health literacy bits, further shedding light on the multiple phases and literacy practices that are embedded within the multifaceted concept of health literacy. Although this research has focused primarily on online health information seeking, these health literacy bits are needed to successfully navigate both print and online sources. There are six phases of health information seeking: (1) Information Need Identification and Question Formulation, (2) Information Search, (3) Information Comprehension, (4) Information Assessment, (5) Information Management, and (6) Information Use.

The first phase is the *information need identification and question formulation phase.* In this phase, one needs to be able to develop and refine a range of questions to frame one's search and understand relevant health terms. In the second phase, *information search,* one has to possess appropriate searching skills, such as using proper keywords and correct spelling in search terms, especially when using search engines and databases. It is also crucial to understand how search engines work (i.e., how search results are derived, what the order of the search results means, how to use the snippets that are provided in the search results list to select websites, and how to determine which listings are ads on a search engine results page). One also has to limit reliance on surface characteristics, such as the design of a website or a book (a website or book that appears to have a lot of information or looks aesthetically pleasant does not necessarily mean it has good information) and language used (a website or book that utilizes jargon, the keywords that one used to conduct the search, or the word "information" does not necessarily indicate it will have good information). The next phase is *information comprehension*, whereby one needs to have the ability to read, comprehend, and recall the information (including textual, numerical, and visual content) one has located from the books and/or online resources.

To assess the credibility of health information (*information assessment* phase), one needs to be able to evaluate information for accuracy, evaluate how current the information is (e.g., when a website was last updated or when a book was published), and evaluate the creators of the source—for example, examine site sponsors or type of sites (.com, .gov, .edu, or .org) or the author of a book (practicing doctor, a celebrity doctor, a patient of a specific disease, etc.) to determine the believability of the person/ organization providing the information. Such credibility perceptions tend to become generalized, so they must be frequently reexamined (e.g., the belief that a specific news agency always has credible health information needs continuous vetting). One also needs to evaluate the credibility of the medium (e.g., television, Internet, radio, social media, and book) and evaluate—not just accept without questioning—others' claims regarding the validity of a site, book, or other specific source of information. At this stage, one has to "make sense of information gathered from diverse sources by identifying misconceptions, main and supporting ideas, con- flicting information, point of view, and biases" (American Association of School Librarians [AASL], 2009, p. 13) and conclude which sources/ information are valid and accurate by using conscious strategies rather than simply using intuitive judgments or "rules of thumb." This phase is the most challenging segment of health information seeking and serves as a determinant of success (or lack thereof) in the information-seeking process. The following section on Sources of Health Information further explains this phase.

The fifth phase is *information management*, whereby one has to orga- nize information that has been gathered in some manner to ensure easy retrieval and use in the future. The last phase is *information use*, in which one will synthesize information found across various resources, draw conclusions, and locate the answer to his or her original question and/ or the content that fulfills the information need. This phase also often involves implementation, such as using the information to solve a health problem; make health-related decisions; identify and engage in behaviors that will help a person to avoid health risks; share the health information found with family members and friends who may benefit from it; and advocate more broadly for personal, family, or community health.

THE IMPORTANCE OF HEALTH LITERACY

The conception of health has moved from a passive view (someone is either well or ill) to one that is more active and process based (someone is working toward preventing or managing disease). Hence, the dominant focus has shifted from doctors and treatments to patients and prevention, resulting in the need to strengthen our ability and confidence (as patients and consumers of health care) to look for, assess, understand, manage, share, adapt, and use health-related information. An individual's health literacy level has been found to predict his or her health status better than age, race, educational attainment, employment status, and income level (National Network of Libraries of Medicine, 2013). Greater health literacy also enables individuals to better communicate with health care providers such as doctors, nutritionists, and therapists, as they can pose more relevant, informed, and useful questions to health care providers. Another added advantage of greater health literacy is better information-seeking skills, not only for health but also in other domains, such as completing assignments for school.

SOURCES OF HEALTH INFORMATION: THE GOOD, THE BAD, AND THE IN-BETWEEN

For generations, doctors, nurses, nutritionists, health coaches, and other health professionals have been the trusted sources of health information. Additionally, researchers have found that young adults, when they have health-related questions, typically turn to a family member who has had firsthand experience with a health condition because of their family member's close proximity and because of their past experience with, and trust in, this individual. Expertise should be a core consideration when consulting a person, website, or book for health information. The credentials and background of the person or author and conflicting interests of the author (and his or her organization) must be checked and validated to ensure the likely credibility of the health information they are conveying. While books often have implied credibility because of the peer-review process involved, self-publishing has challenged this credibility, so qualifications of book authors should also be verified. When it comes to health information, currency of the source must also be examined. When examining health information/studies presented, pay attention to the exhaustiveness of research methods utilized to offer recommendations or conclusions. Small and nondiverse sample size is often—but not always—an indication of reduced credibility. Studies that confuse correlation with causation is another potential issue to watch for. Information seekers must also pay attention to the sponsors of the research studies. For example, if a study is sponsored by manufacturers of drug Y and the study recommends that drug Y is the best treatment to manage or cure a disease, this may indicate a lack of objectivity on the part of the researchers.

The Internet is rapidly becoming one of the main sources of health information. Online forums, news agencies, personal blogs, social media sites, pharmacy sites, and celebrity "doctors" are all offering medical and health information targeted to various types of people in regard to all types of diseases and symptoms. There are professional journalists, citizen journalists, hoaxers, and people paid to write fake health news on various sites that may appear to have a legitimate domain name and may even have authors who claim to have professional credentials, such as an MD. All these sites *may* offer useful information or information that appears to be useful and relevant; however, much of the information may be debatable and may fall into gray areas that require readers to discern credibility, reliability, and biases.

While broad recognition and acceptance of certain media, institutions, and people often serve as the most popular determining factors to assess credibility of health information among young people, keep in mind that there are legitimate Internet sites, databases, and books that publish health information and serve as sources of health information for doctors, other health sites, and members of the public. For example, MedlinePlus (https://medlineplus.gov) has trusted sources on over 975 diseases and conditions and presents the information in easy-to-understand language.

The chart here presents factors to consider when assessing credibility of health information. However, keep in mind that these factors function only as a guide and require continuous updating to keep abreast with the changes in the landscape of health information, information sources, and technologies.

The chart can serve as a guide; however, approaching a librarian about how one can go about assessing the credibility of both print and online health information is far more effective than using generic checklist-type

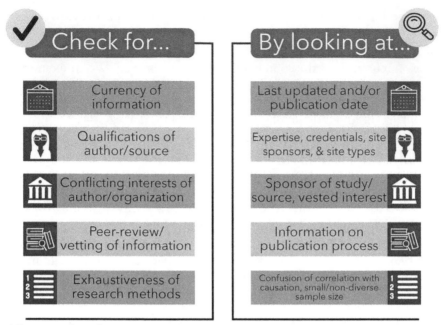

Check for...	By looking at...
Currency of information	Last updated and/or publication date
Qualifications of author/source	Expertise, credentials, site sponsors, & site types
Conflicting interests of author/organization	Sponsor of study/source, vested interest
Peer-review/vetting of information	Information on publication process
Exhaustiveness of research methods	Confusion of correlation with causation, small/non-diverse sample size

All images from flaticon.com

tools. While librarians are not health experts, they can apply and teach patrons strategies to determine the credibility of health information.

With the prevalence of fake sites and fake resources that appear to be legitimate, it is important to use the following health information assessment tips to verify health information that one has obtained (St. Jean et al., 2015, p. 151):

- **Don't assume you are right**: Even when you feel very sure about an answer, keep in mind that the answer may not be correct, and it is important to conduct (further) searches to validate the information.
- **Don't assume you are wrong**: You may actually have correct information, even if the information you encounter does not match—that is, you may be right and the resources that you have found may contain false information.
- **Take an open approach**: Maintain a critical stance by not including your preexisting beliefs as keywords (or letting them influence your choice of keywords) in a search, as this may influence what it is possible to find out.
- **Verify, verify, and verify**: Information found, especially on the Internet, needs to be validated, no matter how the information appears on

the site (i.e., regardless of the appearance of the site or the quantity of information that is included).

Health literacy comes with experience navigating health information. Professional sources of health information, such as doctors, health care providers, and health databases, are still the best, but one also has the power to search for health information and then verify it by consulting with these trusted sources and by using the health information assessment tips and guide shared previously.

Mega Subramaniam, PhD
Associate Professor, College of Information Studies
University of Maryland

REFERENCES AND FURTHER READING

American Association of School Librarians (AASL). (2009). *Standards for the 21st-century learner in action*. Chicago, IL: American Association of School Librarians.

Hilligoss, B., & Rieh, S.-Y. (2008). Developing a unifying framework of credibility assessment: Construct, heuristics, and interaction in context. *Information Processing & Management, 44*(4), 1467–1484.

Kuhlthau, C. C. (1988). Developing a model of the library search process: Cognitive and affective aspects. *Reference Quarterly, 28*(2), 232–242.

National Network of Libraries of Medicine (NNLM). (2013). Health literacy. Bethesda, MD: National Network of Libraries of Medicine. Retrieved from nnlm.gov/outreach/consumer/hlthlit.html

Ratzan, S. C., & Parker, R. M. (2000). Introduction. In C. R. Selden, M. Zorn, S. C. Ratzan, & R. M. Parker (Eds.), *National Library of Medicine current bibliographies in medicine: Health literacy*. NLM Pub. No. CBM 2000–1. Bethesda, MD: National Institutes of Health, U.S. Department of Health and Human Services.

St. Jean, B., Taylor, N. G., Kodama, C., & Subramaniam, M. (2017). Assessing the health information source perceptions of tweens using card-sorting exercises. *Journal of Information Science*. Retrieved from http://journals.sagepub.com/doi/abs/10.1177/0165551516687728

St. Jean, B., Subramaniam, M., Taylor, N. G., Follman, R., Kodama, C., & Casciotti, D. (2015). The influence of positive hypothesis testing on youths' online health-related information seeking. *New Library World, 116*(3/4), 136–154.

Subramaniam, M., St. Jean, B., Taylor, N.G., Kodama, C., Follman, R., & Casciotti, D. (2015). Bit by bit: Using design-based research to improve the health literacy of adolescents. *JMIR Research Protocols*, 4(2), paper e62. Retrieved from http://www.ncbi.nlm.nih.gov/pmc/ articles/PMC4464334/

Valenza, J. (2016, November 26). Truth, truthiness, and triangulation: A news literacy toolkit for a "post-truth" world [Web log]. Retrieved from http://blogs.slj.com/neverendingsearch/2016/11/26/truth-truthi ness-triangulation-and-the-librarian-way-a-news-literacy-toolkit-for-a-post-truth-world/

Common Misconceptions about Self-Injury

1. SELF-INJURY IS ONLY FOUND IN ADOLESCENTS

Though it is most commonly reported in adolescents and young adults, self-harming is something that can strike at any age. While adolescents appear to be the most vulnerable, self-harming has been observed in middle-aged adults and seniors suffering from dementia as well. Case histories of self-harming behavior in children as young as two or three have also been reported as well as in patients suffering from a wide range of neurological and psychiatric disorders. Even for those people who begin self-harming as adolescents, however, the legacy can carry over long into adulthood. Though the reasons that people may have for injuring themselves may change at different stages across the life span, self-harming is something that always needs to be taken seriously. Please refer to Question 4 for more information.

2. GIRLS ARE MORE LIKELY TO HARM THEMSELVES THAN BOYS

Though it is a common misconception that females are more likely to self-harm than males, actual research has shown little or no real difference between male and female self-harmers. But there can still be important difference in the *nature* of the self-harming that does occur. For example, males often harm themselves much more severely than females and are also more likely to take greater health risks, such as not taking proper care of their injuries. Males can also be more prone to self-destructive behavior that can resemble self-harming in many ways, though this is often overlooked due to the belief that "boys will be boys." Not only can this lead to a greater risk of serious injury, but they also run a greater risk of accidental death. Just as importantly, males are less likely to admit that they are harming themselves or to ask for help. Please see Question 3 for further details.

3. IT'S JUST A PLAY FOR ATTENTION

This is a common misconception and a dangerous one, especially for people who can't bring themselves to believe that anyone would deliberately harm themselves unless they wanted attention or were mentally ill. Even when self-harmers admit what they are doing to family or friends, they often get accused of attention seeking, a claim that can be especially hurtful for someone in pain who may be opening up for the first time.

Self-harm attempts may occur for many different reasons, and, yes, that can include trying to call attention to the emotional pain they may be experiencing. Since mental distress is often invisible, creating physical injuries that can be seen by others can be a way of forcing family and friends to recognize what they are going through. Also, when seeking treatment, self-harmers may view doctors and nurses as more likely to consider physical injuries as being more serious than psychological symptoms. In many cases, self-harming may be seen as a "cry for help," which needs to be treated carefully and without judgment. As you can see in Question 10, accusing self-harmers of attention seeking can often backfire tragically.

4. SELF-HARMERS RARELY COMMIT SUICIDE

Even though self-harming and attempted suicide are usually seen as separate mental health issues, they have far more in common than you might think. While self-harmers may not be actively trying to commit suicide, it is still possible for them to kill themselves by accident, whether through cutting too deep and severing an artery or else injuring themselves more severely than expected. Also, many people who harm themselves may simply deny that they are suicidal, out of fear that they might be considered "crazy" and committed to a psychiatric ward. This is why all self-harm attempts need to be assessed by a qualified mental health professional to explore why they are harming themselves and whether future attempts are likely. As the self-harm attempts become more severe, the line between self-harming and deliberate suicidal behavior becomes much easier to cross. Please see Question 7 for more details.

5. SELF-HARMERS SUFFER FROM A PERSONALITY DISORDER

According to the latest edition of the *Diagnostic and Statistical Manual of Mental Disorders* (*DSM-5*), a personality disorder is a long-term pattern of pathological thinking, emotion, behavior, interpersonal functioning, or impulsiveness that can persist along a wide range of personal and social situations. There are many different kinds of personality disorders, and only a qualified mental health professional can make a proper diagnosis. Typically diagnosed in adolescence or young adulthood, personality disorders can develop due to early childhood issues such as child abuse, neglect, early trauma, attachment problems with one or both parents, or social isolation. While self-harming behavior is often associated with certain personality disorders, particularly borderline personality disorder (BPD) or avoidant personality disorder, it can occur for a wide variety of reasons, though people with BPD appear especially vulnerable. Treatment programs that can be highly effective in helping people with personality disorders as well as self-harmers have been developed. See Question 17 for more information.

QUESTIONS AND ANSWERS

General Information

1. What is self-harm?

Coming up with a good definition of self-harm can be difficult given the wide range of different ways that people can inflict physical damage on themselves. The two most commonly used terms are "nonsuicidal self-injury" (or NSSI for short) and "self-harm." These terms can apply to any kind of self-injury that is not meant to be part of a deliberate suicide attempt—in other words, deliberate bodily damage in a way that isn't intended to be fatal.

According to the World Health Organization, deliberate self-harm or NSSI can be defined as "an act with non-fatal outcome in which an individual deliberately initiates a non-habitual behavior, that without intervention from others will cause self-harm, or deliberately ingests a substance in excess of the prescribed or generally recognized therapeutic dosage, and which is aimed at realizing changes that the person desires via the actual or expected physical consequences."

Though the most common form of self-harm involves self-cutting, there are many different methods people can use to harm themselves such as burning, swallowing a harmful substance, head-banging, wall-punching, and the like. Part of the problem in diagnosing self-harm in other cultures is that it can be confused with different forms of body modification (including tattooing and deliberate scarring).

While formally classified as a mental disorder, self-harm or NSSI has been listed in the latest edition of the *Diagnostic and Statistical Manual of Mental Disorders* (*DSM-5*) for possible inclusion as a disorder in future editions. Among the different criteria listed, a diagnosis of self-harm includes:

1. Having at least five incidents of deliberate self-harm in the previous year but with no intention of committing suicide. Self-harm attempts can run the gamut from cutting, bruising the skin, drinking a corrosive or poisonous substance, deliberately inflicting pain, or leaving permanent marks on the skin.
2. The self-injuring occurs in order to relieve negative emotions or thoughts; as a way of dealing with interpersonal problems or stress; or simply to break through the emotional numbing that many trauma victims report.
3. People who injure themselves often experience frequent thoughts about self-injury as well as emotional distress that occur immediately prior to the self-harm attempt. They can also feel a sense of relief afterward due to the psychological rush brought on by giving in to their need to injure themselves.
4. Self-injuries that occur as part of a religious or cultural ritual are not considered to be symptoms of self-harm. This can include body piercing, tattooing, or other forms of body art.
5. The self-injury has to be severe enough to interfere with regular social or occupational functioning. This can be difficult since many self-harmers can keep their behavior hidden, at least in the early stages, though self-harming often becomes more serious with time.

It is also possible for self-harm to occur as a symptom of another mental disorder. This can include self-harm occurring under the influence of drugs or alcohol, during a psychotic episode, or due to an obsessive-compulsive disorder causing compulsive behaviors that might lead to self-harm (e.g., compulsive hair-pulling or head-banging). This is usually more complex since treatment needs to be provided for the other mental symptoms as well as the self-harming.

There are also milder forms of self-harm that may not be considered particularly serious for many people but can still be harmful if taken to extremes. Nail-biting, skin-picking, or head-banging can often occur while people are experiencing deep concentration or feeling bored. Excoriation disorder (skin-picking) is usually found in females who pick at areas of the skin that they consider unsightly or a physical blemish, usually on the face or scalp. Many people who engage in this kind of behavior report feelings of pleasure afterward even if they are aware they are injuring themselves.

Tattooing or body modifications are not considered to be examples of self-harm unless they are done with intention of self-injury (which can be difficult to diagnose). Extreme forms of body modification seen in other cultures are usually not considered to be examples of self-harm either (see Questions 6 and 26).

If you are not certain whether something that you are doing might be considered to be self-harm or not, speak with your family physician or someone you trust.

2. Who are most likely to harm themselves?

At present, it can often be hard to determine just how common self-harming really is, considering most cases are never seen by health professionals and self-harmers often don't seek any kind of help. It can also be difficult to distinguish self-harmers from true suicidal behavior since many people may be genuinely uncertain whether they meant to kill themselves or not. This is why many countries around the world don't have reliable statistics on self-harm attempts.

According to one 2014 American survey, 5.9 percent of all adults have engaged in some form of self-harm in their lives, with 2.7 percent doing it five or more times. For adolescents and young adults, however, the risk of self-harm is much greater, with 12–18 percent reporting some form of self-harm behavior. The likelihood of self-harm also rises for those with various psychological issues such as interpersonal problems, personality disorders, emotional or other mental health problems, cognitive deficits, or being at risk for suicide.

As you can see from these statistics, young people (particularly anyone under the age of 25) are much more prone to self-harm attempts, though they can occur at any age. This is likely due to young people being less emotionally mature than adults and also because adolescence and early adulthood can be an extremely scary time for many people.

As adolescents, we often face substantial social conflicts and pressures as we try to assume adult roles, all of which can often lead to feelings of estrangement from parents and a growing sense of isolation. This stress can lead to greater risk of suicide, substance abuse, and self-harm, particularly for young people believing they have no real support from the people around them. Other problems, such as bullying (whether the face-to-face variety or cyberbullying), can also make it much more difficult to cope, especially if they are part of a sexual minority or otherwise made to feel different from other people of their age. Adolescents suffering from social anxiety and who have difficulty forming friendships or romantic partnerships seem especially prone to self-harm.

People with a history of self-harm attempts often report significant problems with depression and anxiety, impulsiveness, and suicidal thinking and generally tend to have generalized problems with social functioning. They may also have a history of childhood physical or sexual abuse, neglect, or related emotional trauma.

In one recent study published in the journal *Psychological Assessment*, 3,559 undergraduate students from an American university completed an online survey looking at self-harm behavior. The students in the study ranged in age from 18 to 57 (average age of 20). According to the study results, 428 participants (11.7%) reported at least one self-harm act in the previous year.

The researchers also found three distinct groups: the ones who didn't harm themselves at all, the ones who self-harm once in a while (less than five times a year), and the ones who self-harm more frequently (six or more times a year). Though the occasional self-harmers showed greater problems with anxiety, depression, and overall quality of life than the ones who didn't harm themselves, they were still well adjusted than those who harm themselves frequently. In addition, frequent self-harmers showed significant problems with regulating their emotions and were often prone to excessive psychological reactions to stressful situations. Thus, self-harming can often become a coping strategy to handle this intolerable sense of stress and frustration.

Self-harm is also strongly related to personality problems, particularly borderline and avoidant personality disorder, which can become especially apparent during adolescence or young adulthood. Also, self-harm attempts are often seen in prisons and psychiatric hospitals where people may be more prone to act out due to boredom or conflicts with staff or inmates. Patients suffering from brain damage or developmental disorders such as autism may also engage in head-banging, hair-pulling, or other forms of self-harming behavior whenever they are feeling upset or frustrated.

3. Are women more likely to harm themselves than men?

Despite the widespread belief that females are more likely to injure themselves than males, many research studies have shown little or no real difference between male and female self-harmers—at least in terms of how *frequently* self-harm attempts occur. On the other hand, men can often harm themselves much more *severely* than women and are also less likely to take proper care of their injuries. This can mean a greater risk of serious medical complications (including infections) as well as greater risk of killing themselves by accident. They are also less likely to admit that they are harming themselves or to ask for help from family, friends, or medical professionals.

Part of the problem when men harm themselves is that these attempts can often be overlooked or dismissed with statements such as "boys will be boys" or "just guys doing guy stuff". Unexplained cuts or bruises can be passed off as being due to roughhousing with friends, participating in contact sports or other activities where injuries can occur, or simply being clumsy (though admittedly these excuses are becoming more common in females as well). Along with direct self-harm attempts seen in males (attempts in which they *intended* to harm themselves), there can also be *indirect* self-harm behaviors that are much less likely to be seen in women.

Many males enjoy putting themselves in situations where they risk physical harm, or even death, which is often justified as a "need to put it all on the line" rather than a deliberate attempt at self-injury (at least on the surface). This can include involvement in "extreme" sports, unsafe driving, unprotected sex, or excessive drinking or drug abuse. In many cases, they can combine these different activities, and the risk of injury becomes even greater.

Some men can even engage in bizarre "bonding" practices to prove their courage such as smashing beer cans on their forehead, shooting staples into their legs, punching walls (or each other), and even engaging in "dares" or stunts to demonstrate their manhood or to show solidarity with other males. While many of these activities likely wouldn't meet the DSM criteria for self-harm, this need for "thrill seeking" can be linked to problems with expressing thoughts and feelings often associated with what is seen in direct self-harm attempts.

Part of the difficulty surrounding whether men are more prone to self-harm than women is the fact that many kinds of self-harm can be seen as an acceptable form of behavior for some men. This is especially true for younger males who justify acting out this way as being due to the need for an "adrenaline rush" or as a way of impressing potential relationship partners. For younger females, however, any kind of behavior that might lead to them hurting themselves is more likely to be seen as pathological since they often don't have the kind of excuses for their behavior that males do (though, again, this is changing in our modern society).

Many men who self-harm may justify what they do in terms of thrill seeking or winning approval from other males. They can also be using self-harm as a way of demonstrating to others that they are feeling emotionally distressed, something that is often more difficult for men to admit than women.

While self-harm attempts can be serious for anyone, regardless of gender, it is still important to recognize that there can be important differences between the kind of self-harm attempts seen in males and females as well as what is motivating them to harm themselves. Recognizing these differences makes it easier to encourage self-harmers to admit what is happening and to provide them with the help they need.

4. Is it only teenagers who harm themselves?

While self-harming is most commonly seen in adolescents and young adults, it's something that can occur at any age. Cases of self-harming behavior in children as young as five or six (or even earlier) have been reported in the clinical literature, though, admittedly, examples like these are rare. Most of these cases involve children with developmental problems, such as early infantile autism or severe intellectual impairments, who are prone to aggressive outbursts whenever they are frustrated. There are also recognized neurological disorders such as Lesch-Nyhan syndrome that can cause even very young children to injure themselves.

In more common examples of early self-harming behavior, children who have been exposed to early abuse, whether physical, sexual, or emotional, or who deal with parental neglect can begin harming themselves well before puberty. Many of these children also display different forms of antisocial behavior, including fire setting, stealing, bullying, or aggressive acting out. In all cases involving children showing problem behavior at an early age, the possibility of self-harming or even suicidal behavior should always be considered.

But self-harm behavior can be found in older adults as well. A recent study looking at national trends in U.S. hospital admissions for self-harm events (including suicidal and nonsuicidal self-injury) found a significant rise in self-harming among adults aged 45–64 years from 2001 to 2011. This increase appears to be greater than the increase seen for adolescents and young adults. Though, like their younger counterparts, most older self-harmers do their best to conceal what they are doing, hospital admissions are hardly uncommon. Most of these admissions appear to be linked to mental health problems such as depression and reflect similar increases seen in suicide rates for middle-aged adults.

Along with the mental health problems often seen in older self-harmers, researchers have found that seniors suffering from different kinds of dementia, including Alzheimer's disease, also have an elevated risk of self-harm compared to seniors without dementia. According to recent studies, the hospitalization rate for self-harm in individuals over the age of 60 is double the rate for nondementia seniors. Self-harm methods favored by older adults with dementia include self-poisoning or drinking corrosive substances (whether or not suicide was intended), which often occurs at home or in long-term care facilities. Much like "wandering" (another common problem in seniors with dementia), family and care workers need to stay vigilant to prevent this kind of self-injuring behavior.

Along with dementia, other factors that seem to increase the risk of self-harm in seniors include geriatric depression, substance abuse, psychiatric problems, and lack of positive social relationships. Protective factors that lower the risk of self-harm in seniors include being married or having a strong network of friends and family members to prevent depression or loneliness. Seniors placed in nursing homes, often against their will, are also at an increased risk for self-harm. Recent statistics for nursing home patients over the age of 65 suggest that the likelihood of self-harming behavior can be as high as 14 percent. For patients with dementia or who need to be kept isolated because of impulsive behavior, the likelihood of self-harming can be even greater.

As you can see, self-harming behavior is something that can occur at any age, even though most people associate it exclusively with depressed adolescents. While the reasons that people may have for injuring themselves may change as they grow older, encouraging self-harmers to come forward and acknowledge their need to deal with what is happening is still the key to getting better.

5. Are people who harm themselves less sensitive to pain?

Any self-harm attempt, whether it involves cutting, burning, or some other form of deliberate damage to the body, is going to be painful. Though the fear of pain generally encourages us to be careful not to hurt ourselves, this doesn't appear to be as much of a problem for self-harmers who injure themselves on a regular basis. In fact, laboratory studies have shown that self-harmers tend to have significantly greater ability to tolerate pain than noninjurers.

In one 2010 study comparing university-age self-harmers with control subjects, a device known as an *algometer* was used to measure pain by applying steady pressure to the skin. Though self-harmers and noninjurers showed no difference in pain threshold (the amount of pressure needed to induce the feeling of pain), self-harmers were able to tolerate pain significantly longer than the control subjects. Similar results were found using other methods of inflicting pain under laboratory conditions such as mild electric shocks and placing an arm in cold water.

But this still leaves the question of *why* self-harmers have such a high pain tolerance. While some researchers have pointed out that people with emotional problems also show a high tolerance for pain (since emotional turmoil can take our minds off pain we are feeling), self-harmers are able to tolerate pain even when emotional problems such as anxiety, depression, and hopelessness have been taken into consideration.

One hypothesis proposed by psychologist Thomas Joiner is that people who engage in self-harm become gradually desensitized to pain. He also suggests that the sense of emotional relief that follows self-harm attempts may act as a reinforcement that makes future self-harm attempts more likely.

Another intriguing possibility has been raised by Jill M. Hooley of Harvard University. Through extensive interviews with self-harmers, she and her colleagues have noticed that people who self-harm often have extremely negative opinions about themselves, leading them to believe that they *deserve* to be punished. Hooley and her colleagues argue that this innate need for punishment allows self-harmers to tolerate pain much longer than noninjurers, something that research studies tend to support. One typical study conducted in 2013 found that even a brief treatment session helping self-harmers feel better about themselves can lead to their being less able to tolerate pain under laboratory conditions.

Another study published in 2014 showed that self-harmers who report feeling a need to punish themselves often report far greater pain tolerance than people who harm themselves for other reasons. No other differences between these two groups of self-harmers were found in terms of how often they harm themselves or whether they wanted to stop their self-injuring behavior. The researchers also found that people who feel that they deserve to be punished become more desensitized to pain over time, making them more likely to injure themselves in future.

Though it still isn't clear why self-harmers can become desensitized to pain, this often leads to self-harm attempts becoming more severe over time so that self-harmers can get the same emotional release that less severe attempts once provided for them. Of course, greater pain tolerance also has drawbacks. This need to harm themselves more severely can lead to a legacy of bodily damage that can last a lifetime—all the more reason to get help as soon as possible.

6. How far back in history does self-harm go?

Archeologists have found evidence of deliberate self-mutilation in virtually every human culture and even well into prehistory. As far back as the fifth century BC, Greek writers described how war leaders often sliced their flesh before going into battle so that their blood could be used as an offering to the gods for victory. Many shamans and tribal warriors in early societies scarred themselves as a test of manhood or as part of religious ceremonies so they could be purified. Traditional self-mutilation often involved slicing or removing body parts, circumcision, removing teeth, or modifying their bodies in other ways.

In different tribal societies, young men often underwent special rites of passage in which they were expected to undergo ritual mutilation without protest to show their courage. For example, high-ranking Maori of New Zealand undergo a process known as "ta moko" in which elaborate patterns are carved on their face and body using a series of special chisels. Though use of ta moko had declined in the 20th century, it is undergoing a resurgence as young Maori are rediscovering their cultural heritage. There are other examples of extreme body modification found in many cultures, which seem to be gaining popularity as a way of honoring past traditions.

Even in the Bible, there are passages telling believers to pluck out their eyes or castrate themselves to avoid being led into sin. Throughout the history of the early Catholic Church, there are numerous examples of religious people deliberately mutilating themselves in various ways to show their devotion and to suppress any sexual feelings they might have. This often ranged from the wearing of hair shirts, self-flagellation (whipping), extreme fasting, and self-mutilation. Though the Church never officially condoned these practices, many of these self-mutilators were later proclaimed as saints after their death.

Beginning in the 19th century, mental health professionals began taking a closer look at self-harming behavior and what motivated people to inflict injuries on themselves. Though usually reported in psychiatric patients, self-harming could occur in nonpatients as well. In the last half of the 1800s, medical doctors began reporting on a strange fad occurring among young women in different parts of Europe. For no apparent reason, these women would insert numerous pins and needles into different parts of their body (which earned them the popular name of "needle girls"). Though medical doctors suggested that needle girls suffered from hysteria (a common diagnosis for women in the 18th and 19th centuries), treating this need for self-harm was often difficult. This particular fad slowly faded as the 20th century began, but medical cases of men and women deliberately harming themselves continued to be reported in the medical literature.

It was psychiatrist Karl Menninger who first coined the term "self-mutilation" to describe what he was seeing in many of his patients and to distinguish them from suicide cases. While other medical doctors also reported on self-harming behavior in their patients, getting accurate statistics on how frequently this occurred was often next to impossible since most self-harmers preferred not to seek medical help.

Beginning in the 1960s and continuing through to the 1980s, research studies describing what was often called the "wrist-cutting syndrome" became more common. Unfortunately, the studies being reported all dealt with patients being treated in hospital inpatient programs, and the only ones really aware of them were the mental health professionals who were treating them. Also, for the most part, these studies focused primarily on women who were considered to be most likely to harm themselves.

In those pre-Internet days, self-injurers were often afraid of seeking help for fear that they would be considered "crazy" (a legitimate fear since many medical professionals had little real information to go on in assessing and treating self-harmers who came to them). This meant that self-harmers often needed to suffer in silence with few opportunities for helpful advice. While this is slowly changing as better information becomes available, it will likely take time for self-harmers everywhere to gain the confidence they need to admit that they need help.

7. Is self-harm the same as attempted suicide?

While self-harming and attempted suicide are usually seen as separate mental health issues, the difference is not as obvious as you might think. Even for those self-harmers who are not actively trying to commit suicide, it is still possible to kill themselves by accident, whether through cutting too deep and severing an artery or else injuring themselves more severely than expected.

Many people found to be harming themselves may also deny that they had intended to commit suicide for fear of being considered "crazy" and committed to a mental hospital for observation (which continues to be a distinct possibility in many places). This is why all self-harmers should be assessed by a qualified mental health professional to explore why they are harming themselves and whether future attempts are likely.

Even if there is no actual intent of committing suicide, self-harm is often a strong predictor of future suicide risk. While depression or having a history of suicide attempts can also be suicide predictors, research suggests that self-harm attempts may well be one of the best predictors of all. Studies of young people who have committed suicide often show that they have a prior history of deliberately hurting themselves, whether or not these previous attempts were classified as self-harm. Psychological autopsies examining young people who died by suicide have shown anywhere from one-fourth to two-thirds of these victims had attempted some form of self-harm prior to their deaths.

One intriguing theory for explaining the link between self-harm and suicide attempts is Thomas Joiner's interpersonal theory of suicide. According to this theory, people who attempt to kill themselves must not only wish to end their lives but also need to acquire what Joiner called a *capability* for suicide. This means being able to overcome the natural sense of self-preservation we all have, something that usually occurs due to various painful and provocative experiences (PPE) throughout their lives. People who have been severely abused as children, who have experienced or witnessed serious violence, who develop relationship problems or experience bullying, or who have survived traumatic events often become more desensitized to pain and the prospect of death.

Repeated self-harm attempts can also be an important PPE in their own right by desensitizing self-harmers to pain and the threat of injury. Research studies have confirmed that people who engage in self-harm have a significantly reduced fear of death compared to non-self-harmers.

Two other factors mentioned by Joiner in his theory are *perceived burdensomeness* or the belief that one's continuing existence represents a burden to family and friends and *social alienation* or a low sense of belonging to something larger, whether it is a family, a circle of friends, or some other social group that is considered valuable. Joiner suggests that the desire for suicide stems from the interaction of these different factors.

While it is still unclear how well Joiner's theory applies to self-harmers specifically, there is a strong possibility that, over time, the dividing line between self-harm and deliberate suicide intent can become much easier for self-harmers who have simply learned not to care whether they survive their self-harm attempt. This relates to a second theory known as the gateway theory. In this theory, self-harm behavior can be seen as a "gateway" to later suicide as self-harm attempts continue to escalate. For this reason, all self-harm attempts need to be taken seriously whenever they occur, regardless of whether or not there was any actual intention of suicide.

8. What are some of the different methods used by self-harmers?

The kind of self-harm behaviors people can engage in can cover a wide range of different options depending on what is available to self-harmers and how extensive the damage they inflict on themselves can be. Self-harm behaviors can include:

- Scratching using finger nails, paper clips, razor blades, or other common household objects to abrade the skin, often to the point of drawing blood. Some self-harmers even attempt do-it-yourself tattoos to create permanent designs on their skin. These are most often found on the arms, legs, or abdomen, in places that can be easily concealed. This kind of self-harm typically heals with time, though some scratching can be severe enough to be permanent.

- Picking at scabs, pimples, birthmarks, or other points on the skin to the point of breaking the skin and drawing blood. There is also a psychological disorder known as excoriation or skin-picking disorder, which involves repeatedly scratching or picking points on the skin to remove perceived imperfections in the skin. This is usually considered to be a separate condition rather than a form of self-harm.

- Rubbing the skin using fingertips or some common object such as a pencil or an eraser. Repeated rubbing can lead to burning or abrasions along with pain and bleeding and, like self-cutting or scratching, can also lead to permanent scarring if severe enough.

- The most common form of self-harm involves cutting the skin. This can range from light slicing to deep gashes that require medical treatment. As with scratching or abrading the skin, these cuts are usually found on the arms (especially around the wrists), legs, or abdomen. Cutting is also most likely to leave permanent scars on the skin, which need to be kept concealed. People who cut themselves may have a preferred method such as using a particular tool, though many self-harmers simply rely on whatever is available. Though the cutting is usually not intended as an actual suicide attempt, many self-harmers can "play with" the idea of suicide depending on where the cuts are located and how deep the cuts go. Also, as the cuts become more severe, the risk of accidental death becomes greater.

- Burning the skin can also be common with self-harmers. This can involve friction burns with a household object such as an eraser or sandpaper being rubbed vigorously across the skin or actual burning of the skin using lit cigarettes, a cigarette lighter, or a hot iron or stove. In extreme cases, people have been known to harm themselves using fire from a blowtorch or hot coals from a barbecue.

- Hanging or self-strangulation (when not used as a deliberate suicide attempt or for autoerotic asphyxiation). Usually it involves strangulation with a belt or strip of cloth with enough "give" to avoid serious injury or death.

- Breaking bones by punching walls, deliberately jumping from a high place (but not enough to be lethal), or even breaking bones with a hammer. Head-bangers can also be included in this category, though, while risking concussion, there usually isn't enough force to fracture the skull.

- Ingesting a harmful substance such as a household-cleaning fluid. Again, this can be hard to tell apart from an actual suicide attempt since many self-harmers may not be certain how toxic the substance they are taking actually is. Some self-harmers may even try swallowing objects with sharp edges such as needles, razor blades, glass fragments, or pins. Though there is a psychiatric condition called pica that involves compulsive swallowing of nonorganic substances such as paper, hair, paint chips, paper clips, and the like, this usually isn't regarded as a form of self-harm since self-injury rarely occurs. Some addicts also engage in solvent abuse, or "sniffing" gasoline, glue, or other substances to get high. While this is also potentially dangerous, it is treated as a form of addiction rather than as self-harm.

While many self-harmers may limit themselves to one favorite method, others may try to harm themselves in different ways. Ultimately though, self-harm is self-harm regardless of the method people decide to use. What really matters is how severe the damage inflicted is, how frequently self-harm attempts occur, and why the self-harm occurred in the first place.

9. What reasons do people give for harming themselves?

According to the four-function model of self-harm proposed by Matthew Nock and Mitchell Prinstein, there appear to be four main motivations for self-harm:

- Automatic positive reinforcement—self-harm intended to produce a positive emotional or mental state, for example, the emotional "high" that can occur after a self-cutting episode. This may be linked to the body's production of endorphins whenever an injury occurs (see Question 11).
- Automatic negative reinforcement—self-harm as a way of escaping from negative emotions or relieving tension, for example, self-injuring when feeling frustrated or rejected.
- Social positive reinforcement—self-harm in order to seek help and make important life changes, for example, self-harming to alert friends or family how serious things have become.
- Social negative reinforcement—self-harm as a way of escaping from toxic social situations, for example, self-harming to avoid bullies.

The use of the term "automatic" describes how the physical emotions and sensations that self-harmers experience directly help reinforce the self-harming behavior, while "social" means that the self-harm is meant to influence how they interact with the world around them.

When asked directly why they are hurting themselves, self-harmers can provide all sorts of reasons for what is happening, which often reflect the motivations pointed out by Nock and Prinstein. Some of the reasons they can give include:

- Feeling lonely or unwanted (automatic negative reinforcement)
- As a "cry for help" to let the people around them know that they are experiencing emotional pain (social positive reinforcement)
- To punish themselves for something they did that makes them feel guilty (automatic negative reinforcement)
- To distract them from other problems they may be facing (social negative reinforcement)
- To release emotional or physical tension (automatic negative reinforcement)
- Because they were feeling overwhelmed by the problems they were facing (automatic negative reinforcement)

- So they could feel in control of their life. Many self-harmers argue that hurting themselves allows them to experience pain in a way that is easier to deal with than the other kinds of emotional pain they are facing (a combination of both automatic positive and negative reinforcement)
- Believing that, if they hurt themselves, they will become more used to pain and be better able to handle whatever other people do to them (a combination of both automatic positive and negative reinforcement)
- In order to feel something or, for self-harmers dealing with other kinds of pain, to numb themselves (automatic positive reinforcement)

For many self-harmers, especially self-harmers who are adolescents or pre-adolescents, there is often a sense that, if they don't harm themselves, then they will "explode" because of their unexpressed emotions. Cutting or burning allows this inner pain to come to the surface where they can deal with it in concrete ways that are easier to understand.

According to a 2016 study examining different motives for self-harm in adolescent boys and girls, reasons for self-harm were classified as intrapersonal (dealing with internal emotional states) or interpersonal (resulting from their relationships with other people). Overall, intrapersonal motives were far more common with statements such as "I wanted to get relief from a terrible state of mind" being far more likely to be endorsed than statements such as "I wanted to find out if someone really loved me." People reporting intrapersonal motives were found to be 17 times more likely to harm themselves again over the six-month follow-up period.

That same study also found significant gender differences in self-harm motivations. Girls were far more likely than boys to describe their self-harm attempt as being due to wanting to die. On the other hand, boys were far more likely to describe their self-harm attempt as being a deliberate attempt at frightening the people around them.

Though self-harmers can report numerous different reasons for wanting to harm themselves, the most common motivation seems to be coming to terms with psychological pain. Understanding what inspires people to harm themselves is a vital first step in the process of providing treatment.

10. Do people harm themselves just to get attention?

This is a question that often gets asked. For many people, it is often impossible to believe that anyone would deliberately harm themselves unless they are seeking attention. Considering the obvious pain that comes with repeated self-injury, self-harmers frequently face this kind of disbelief when they are admitting what is happening to family or friends, especially if the self-harm has been going on for some time. But accusing a self-harmer of simply wanting attention can have serious consequences, especially for someone in real pain who may be opening up to someone else for the first time.

As you have seen previously, self-harm attempts may occur for many different reasons. According to the model of deliberate self-harm covered in a previous section, people can injure themselves as a way of escaping toxic situations by bringing internal pain out into the open. Since mental distress is often invisible, creating physical injuries that can be seen by others can be a way of forcing family and friends to recognize what they are going through. Self-harmers may consider the physical suffering that comes with self-harming as being more "legitimate" than emotional suffering and easier to deal with (if only by slapping on a bandage). Also, in terms of seeking medical attention, self-harmers may view doctors and nurses as tending to take physical injuries more seriously than psychological symptoms.

For people dealing with abuse, whether in the form of being bullied or through physical and sexual abuse from a parent or caregiver, self-harm may become a way of forcing police and health care professionals to take their complaints more seriously. Also, if they are feeling trapped in an unhappy home life or relationship, engaging in self-harm often becomes a "cry for help" to force the other people in their life to pay attention to what is happening as well as to take control over their own lives.

A clear example of this can be found in a memorable 1995 interview with British journalist Martin Bashir when Princess Diana candidly admitted to injuring herself on her arms and legs. In that interview, she stated, "You have so much pain inside yourself that you try and hurt yourself on the outside because you want help." Many other self-harmers have reported similar sentiments in media interviews as well.

It's also important to remember that many people who harm themselves go to extreme lengths to keep it secret. Even when the injuries become severe enough to require emergency medical treatment, self-harmers often refuse to admit that they have a problem and may try inventing implausible excuses for whatever scars they may have. If they have reached the stage of wanting to admit their self-harm, this should be treated as a potential breakthrough since it can also mean that they admit to having a problem and are ready to seek treatment.

While more self-harmers than ever are coming forward to seek help, too many others prefer to stay in the shadows due to the stigma that often comes with admitting that they are hurting themselves. So rather than accusing self-harmers of being attention seekers, it is far better to be as nonjudgmental as possible as you explore the different reasons they may have for injuring themselves. Gaining trust is the only way to convince self-harmers to take that next step toward seeking treatment.

11. Can self-harming be addictive?

This can be a difficult question to answer in many ways. Although most self-harmers can give different reasons for why they are harming themselves (see Question 9), there can be physiological factors at work as well, which researchers are just beginning to understand.

For example, cutting, tearing, or otherwise damaging skin stimulates nerve endings and creates the sensation of pain. This in turn causes the brain to release endorphins in the brain and bloodstream. Endorphins are brain chemicals that are similar in structure to heroin and cocaine and can lead to a psychological "high" that can last as long as 15 or 20 minutes. While most commonly associated with pain, vigorous exercise or other high-intensity activities can trigger the release of endorphins as well—hence the familiar sensation of the "runner's high" following a lengthy workout.

Whatever the trigger, the sense of euphoria that results from increased endorphins in the body can boost the body's ability to handle pain. One problem for self-harmers is that frequent endorphin release can also lead to greater pain tolerance over time as the body builds up a partial immunity to endorphins. This means that future self-harm attempts may not lead to the same kind of "high" experienced before as the body adapts to the added endorphin production.

Much like drug addicts who develop a tolerance for heroin or cocaine, self-harmers may need to injure themselves much more severely to get the same emotional release they got from less serious wounds in the past. Thus, a vicious cycle of more and more severe self-harm attempts begins as they become less sensitive to pain (see Question 5).

But is it possible for self-harmers to become addicted to pain the way that addicts can become addicted to narcotics? A 2011 study conducted by researchers at Oxford University examined self-harm in more than 11,000 people who were treated for self-harm attempts between 1993 and 2006. What the study researchers found was that people with drug abuse problems were far more likely to harm themselves over a 12-month period. They were also more likely to be younger, to have related alcohol problems, and to have emotional problems that often contribute to their need to self-harm in the first place.

In exploring whether self-harm is addictive, we need to consider what addiction actually means. *Physical addiction* refers to the body forming a dependence on a given substance such as alcohol or narcotics, often to the point of developing severe withdrawal effects if someone tries to quit "cold turkey." On the other hand, it is also possible to form a psychological dependence with the addictive substance, or even specific behaviors such as gambling become an essential part of someone's ability to cope with stress or emotional problems.

Though no real evidence exists of withdrawal effects occurring in chronic self-harmers who try to stop, many of these same self-harmers often report psychological distress due to being unable to harm themselves. Since the self-harming often becomes an essential coping strategy for many people, whether to deal with stress or to release internal emotions that build up with time, it can certainly be regarded as a form of psychological dependence. This is also why chronic self-harmers have such difficulty overcoming the self-harm habit and learning more positive ways to handle their life problems. This is why it is so important to remain patient and not giving in to frustration when the self-harming habit seems so hard to break.

12. Is there a self-harm epidemic?

Why are so many new self-harm cases being reported, and where are they all coming from? Many countries around the world report a sharp rise in hospital admissions involving young people, particularly adolescents, who need treatment following self-harm attempts. In the United Kingdom, for example, the National Health Service has recorded 28,730 hospital admissions among 10–19-year-olds with self-harm injuries in 2013/2014. This is up from 22,978 in the previous 12 months, a 25 percent increase.

In Canada, a report from the Canadian Institute of Health Information showed that 2,500 youth were hospitalized for self-harm attempts in 2014—up from 1,300 in 2009–2010. And this same rising trend is being seen in many other countries around the world.

Recognizing this influx of new self-harm cases, more news articles than ever are coming out about self-harming behavior, particularly in adolescents and young adults. Teachers' groups, community health agencies, and mental health organizations are increasingly focusing on self-harming while trying to explain where this epidemic is coming from. But is this really an epidemic, or are we simply becoming more aware of a problem that has always existed? As you can see from Question 6, self-harm has been around for a *very* long time, but there are many different reasons why self-harmers have become more visible than ever.

Until relatively recently, people who harmed themselves often had no source of information available to advise them about where to get help. Since most self-harmers often saw themselves as "freaks" considering that they didn't know of anyone else engaging in that kind of behavior, they were naturally reluctant to tell anyone about what was happening for fear of being thought "crazy." When they tried telling a friend or parent what was happening, the people they trusted with their secret were often as in the dark about what to do as they were themselves.

Even health care professionals such as doctors or nurses who dealt with self-harming patients were often unable to do anything except treat the injuries and try referring their patients to whatever mental health treatment happened to be available. Unfortunately, in many cases there were no treatment programs or trained mental health professionals able to help except possibly in the larger cities. Almost inevitably, an alarming number of misconceptions about self-harm have taken root and continue to be shared by well-meaning people unaware of the potential dangers linked to spreading misconceptions (some examples are provided in earlier sections).

With the rise of the Internet, not to mention better training for medical and mental health professionals, self-harmers now have access to more information than ever about what is happening to them and how they can be treated. Not only are there online websites established by professional counselors and medical organizations, but we are also seeing the growth of online communities of self-harmers, many of whom allow people in need to reach out in ways they never could before. In the References section, there are numerous examples of online sites that permit anyone to learn more about self-harming and where to find needed treatment. Not only are these sites aimed at self-harmers themselves, but they also allow parents, teachers, and medical professionals to educate themselves on self-harming behavior and provide real support to those who need it.

Also, as you can see in the Introduction, numerous celebrities, including Johnny Depp, Fiona Apple, Angelina Jolie, Courtney Love, and Princess Diana, have come forward with their own stories giving self-harm a higher profile than ever. As more self-harmers are becoming aware that they are not alone and that the resources they need are out there, they are becoming more willing than ever to admit what is happening and seek help before it is too late.

---◆❖◆---

Causes and Risk Factors

13. Is self-harm linked to trauma?

While research suggests that self-harm attempts are most likely to occur as a way of relieving emotional distress and negative emotions such as fear, emptiness, loneliness, and sadness, it still isn't clear what can cause these problems and why they might lead to self-harm in the first place. Early trauma, particularly trauma due to childhood physical, emotional, or sexual abuse, is often seen as the most common explanation, though there are many other possibilities as well.

Over the past decade, numerous research studies have linked self-harm behaviors to posttraumatic stress and how people cope with their traumatic memories. Symptoms of posttraumatic stress can include intrusive memories of traumatic events, flashbacks, nightmares, acute stress, and avoidance behavior, though every case is different in terms of the kind of symptoms that can appear and how severe those symptoms are.

The type of traumatic experiences that can lead to posttraumatic stress can also vary from exposure to a life-threatening event (e.g., natural disaster or violence) as well as emotionally devastating experiences such as childhood physical or sexual abuse or exposure to domestic violence. While not everyone having these experiences is going to develop posttraumatic symptoms, self-harm behavior can often occur as a way of coping with traumatic stress when nothing else seems to work.

Interestingly enough, self-harm behavior seems most commonly linked to *dissociative symptoms* often found in posttraumatic stress survivors. Dissociation is a way of coping with stress that involves a partial or total detachment from reality. Falling on a spectrum from mild to more severe forms of dissociation, symptoms can include depersonalization (feeling detached from one's body or that the world around them is dreamlike), psychological numbing (deliberately suppressing emotions or inner feelings), disengagement (apathy or lack of caring about anything taking place around them), and even complete or partial suppression of distressing memories.

While dissociation can help people cope with distressing memories or emotions, the emotional numbing or apathy that comes with it often feels disturbing as well. In many cases, self-harm attempts may be used as a way of breaking through this sense of numbing. It's hardly surprising that many self-harmers report "wanting to feel something" as one of their main motivations for hurting themselves.

The idea of using self-harm to break through the emotional numbing that comes with trauma has even become part of our popular culture. Anyone familiar with Trent Reznor's classic song "Hurt" can recall the opening lyrics: "I hurt myself today/To see if I still feel."

One recent U.S. survey found that 4.3 percent of American adults reported some form of self-harm behavior in the previous six months, while 32 percent reported at least one traumatic experience at some point in their lives. While there was also evidence of a link between self-harm and having symptoms of depression and posttraumatic stress, it was people reporting symptoms of dissociation who were most likely to report engaging in self-harm behavior.

Different therapeutic approaches found to be effective in treating posttraumatic symptoms also seem to help in treating nonsuicidal self-injury. These different treatment methods can include group and individual psychotherapy as well as psychiatric medications for patients with posttraumatic and depressive symptoms. For people who feel the need to harm themselves as a way of coping with trauma, admitting what they are doing to themselves is often the first step in getting the right treatment.

14. Are self-harm attempts caused by being bullied?

As we have already seen, self-harm attempts are often linked to emotional distress associated with early childhood trauma. But there can be other factors at work as well.

In many cases, finding a clear reason for self-harm attempts isn't easy, and many self-harmers can even report difficulty remembering *why* the self-harm started in the first place. Though early childhood problems may have left them more vulnerable to emotional difficulties, it is important to remember that puberty and adolescence is an extremely scary time for most young people. The need to form social relationships, gain friends and acceptance, and, eventually, form romantic attachments and prepare for adulthood can be highly stressful, even for people who have had a good childhood and strong family support.

For young people with a history of poor social behavior, chronic emotional problems, minimal family support, and a sense of being an outsider with others their own age, the risk of developing problems such as depression and suicide can be even greater. Unfortunately, this can often make them more vulnerable to being bullied as well.

Bullying can occur in many different ways. Usually defined as the use of threats, force, or emotional coercion to intimidate or dominate others, bullying behavior can be found just about anywhere humans are known to gather. Whether it happens in schools, neighborhoods, or even online, bullies often target people (usually adolescents) who stand out in some way, whether due to racial or ethnic differences, physical differences such as obesity, or because they belong to a sexual minority.

Many schools, neighborhoods, and workplaces can even have a "culture of bullying" allowing the abuse to continue unchallenged, sometimes for whole generations. Along with the sense of helplessness bullying victims often experience, they can also develop poor self-esteem, antisocial behavior, and emotional problems such as depression and social anxiety. As for the long-term consequences of bullying, research suggests that victims can continue to report symptoms of posttraumatic stress and mental health problems similar to trauma even many years after the bullying stopped.

Research studies looking at the impact of peer bullying on adolescents have shown that being bullied can play a much greater role than childhood sexual or physical abuse in whether young people develop suicidal thoughts or engage in self-harm behavior. As you might expect, young people who report being bullied also report significant problems with depression, which can lead to greater risk of self-harm and other high-risk behaviors.

One factor that seems to play an important role in whether victims of bullying will go on to harm themselves or develop emotional problems deals with the kind of support young people receive from their parents. Young people reporting strong parental support are often more insulated from the devastating emotional impact that bullying can have.

Unfortunately, many children may feel isolated and alone, whether due to having a poor relationship with their parents or because they are being bullied over matters they don't feel comfortable sharing with family, such as their sexual orientation. Young people already dealing with other trauma in their lives, such as sexual abuse, may find themselves turning to self-harm attempts when confronted with bullying as well.

While people can injure themselves for different reasons, it is important to take a closer look at what is happening around them to understand *why* the self-harm is happening. Not everyone exposed to bullying will necessarily harm themselves, but young people who find themselves dealing with the stress associated with being bullied may well find that nothing else will help them cope as well. This is especially true if they don't feel they have any real alternative or don't have the emotional support they need at home.

For teachers, counselors, or friends who suspect someone is self-harming, it is often important to provide the unconditional support needed to help him or her overcome his or her own sense of isolation and admit to what is happening.

15. Can peer pressure lead to self-harm attempts?

One of the most alarming facts about suicide is that it often occurs in clusters. Usually referred to as "copycat suicides," these new deaths can follow shortly after the suicide of someone who is well known to a larger community such as in a school. Young people who are particularly vulnerable to suicidal thoughts or feelings may well decide to identify with the person who committed the first suicide and copy that death as much as possible.

According to the concept of *social contagion*, seeing someone who is part of a social group engaging in a certain behavior may increase the likelihood of that behavior being imitated by other members of that same group. This can apply to popular "memes," including new hairstyles, new fashions in clothing, and patterns of speech such as slang, and can also apply to drug and alcohol abuse, unsafe sex, or other forms of dangerous behavior that can become widely copied because the "cool kids" are doing it. Social contagion can also apply to suicidal behavior, especially if young people are experiencing the same mental health problems as the person being imitated.

And it may not even involve someone they knew personally. During the 1930s, Japan saw a bizarre suicide epidemic involving people throwing themselves into the Mount Mihara volcano near Tokyo.

The epidemic began with the suicide death of a young girl following an unhappy love affair. After her suicide note was published in newspapers across the country, other young people, and even couples who believed that their relationship was doomed, decided to follow that first example. This wave of suicides was only stopped after the Japanese government put up a fence to prevent easy access and made it illegal to purchase one-way tickets to the island where the volcano was located. Even certain locations such as San Francisco's Golden Gate Bridge and the Bloor Viaduct in Toronto have gained reputations as "suicide magnets," and special guardrails have been installed to prevent further copycat deaths. Japan's Aokigahara Forest near Tokyo continues to have a sinister reputation for this reason, and signs have been posted around the area to prevent deaths from occurring.

Newspapers around the world have established special guidelines about how suicides are reported out of fear that high-profile news stories about celebrity suicides might inspire copycat deaths. Also, many schools have implemented suicide protocols to provide counseling to students following a student suicide to ensure that vulnerable young people might get the help they need to prevent further deaths.

But can this apply to self-harming behavior as well? Highly vulnerable young people dealing with problems such as depression, bullying, and family abuse often associate with one another as a form of mutual support. This can also mean sharing "tips" on methods of coping that have been found to be effective, such as self-injury. Some young people may even find themselves being pressured by other members of this group to injure themselves to prove they "belong."

While actual research showing how social contagion can lead to self-harm behavior is still rare, there have been several studies done to date. A 2008 study examining nearly 2,000 college students found that young people who knew someone who self-harmed or who self-harmed and attempted suicide were significantly more likely to harm themselves than those who had no such exposure.

Considering the sharp rise in reported cases of self-harm over the past few years, we may be seeing the effect of social contagion resulting from greater media exposure and more news stories about self-harm than ever. News stories about well-known figures admitting to self-harm behavior maybe playing a role as well. While the greater attention self-harm is receiving can be important for encouraging young people to come forward to ask for help, mental health professionals who work with people who self-harm also need to take social contagion into account to understand why this self-harm is happening.

16. Is self-harm linked to drug or alcohol abuse?

It's probably no coincidence that people who self-harm are prone to drug and alcohol abuse as well. Since self-harm and substance abuse can both help cope with tension, dealing with emotional problems that are hard to control may well lead people to experiment with different coping methods before deciding on the one that will work best for them. In many cases, that may mean relying on more than one method, including self-harming and drug or alcohol abuse, to handle what they are going through.

Substance abuse can take many different forms for many people depending on what happens to be available. Along with alcohol, many adolescents and young adults may begin smoking tobacco as well as less legal substances, including illegally purchased prescription drugs and other kinds of "street drugs" such as crack and ecstasy.

According to one popular hypothesis proposed by psychiatrists Edward Khantzian and Mark Albanese, many people begin using drugs and alcohol as a form of *self-medication* to relieve or change painful mental states. Whether due to early trauma, poor self-esteem, relationship problems, or as a way of coping with unhappiness, different addictive substances can have different effects, and users may often experiment before finding something that "works" for them.

Given the drug culture that often permeates many schools and neighborhoods, particularly in high-crime areas, substance abuse remains a continuing problem in most cities. As a result, people dealing with emotional difficulties linked to self-harm are often strongly motivated to experiment with drugs and alcohol to keep these emotions in check. In much the same way, people searching for a way to handle emotions may turn to self-harm behavior and, depending on how effective they consider it to be, may use it as a form of self-medication as well.

Since alcohol remains the most popular form of substance abuse, as well as being legal in most places, the majority of research studies looking at substance abuse and self-harm have focused on alcohol alone. Many studies looking at college students have shown that 60–70 percent of males and females in college have used alcohol, while 25 percent admitted to current or past self-harming as well. This same research has also shown that alcohol is a strong risk factor for self-harm, and students with a self-harm history are also more likely to report alcohol abuse.

While research looking at drug abuse and self-harm tends to be less common, many studies indicate illicit drug abuse can also be linked to self-harm attempts in adolescents and young adults. A 2009 study of 320 Canadian university students showed that self-harm was fairly common, with

29.4 percent reporting at least one episode of self-injury. The study also showed that illicit drug abuse in the previous year proved to be a significant predictor of past or present self-harm attempts. Even compared to other factors such as history of sexual abuse, binge drinking, and physical neglect, the link between drug abuse and self-harm remained extremely strong.

The connection between substance abuse and self-harm seems particularly elevated in high-risk adolescents and young adults, particularly if they are also dealing with long-term personality problems and mental health issues such as depression. Even for adolescents who "grow out" of self-harming as they become older, the likelihood of developing severe substance abuse problems later in life remains extremely high.

When dealing with self-harmers, health professionals need to screen for substance abuse issues in addition to other mental health concerns that may be contributing to the self-harm attempts. There are also specialized treatment programs for self-harmers who abuse drugs or alcohol.

17. Do people who harm themselves suffer from a personality disorder?

According to the *Diagnostic and Statistical Manual of Mental Disorders-5* (*DSM-5*), a personality disorder is a long-standing and maladaptive behavior pattern that can cause long-term difficulties in social functioning or the ability to be a participating member of society. Typically diagnosed in late adolescence or early adulthood, the roots of this kind of behavior problem often date back to early childhood.

While there are a number of different personality disorder diagnoses, one which has been particularly linked to self-harming behavior is borderline personality disorder (BPD). This is defined as a chronic pattern of abnormal behavior characterized by a history of unstable relationships, fear of abandonment, a poor sense of identity, impulsive behavior, and oversensitivity to criticism and rejection. Symptoms of BPD usually begin sometime between puberty and early adulthood, though, considering how much BPD can resemble other mental health problems seen in high-risk youths, most cases aren't diagnosed until they become adults.

Self-harm and suicide attempts are commonly found in people with BPD, and the *DSM-5* lists self-harm behavior as one of the key symptoms needed for a BPD diagnosis. Around 70 percent of all people with BPD admit to harming themselves at some point in their lives, while 3–10 percent will eventually commit suicide. About two-thirds of all adults with BPD report that their self-harming began while they were teenagers.

While it's hard to say how common BPD really is, some estimates put it at about 1–2 percent of the general population, though people with BPD are often overrepresented among people with mental health problems such as depression and anxiety disorders.

Like many other mental disorders, there is no clear reason why people may develop BPD in the first place. While some research studies suggest that brain abnormalities and genetics can play a role in BPD symptoms, a history of childhood trauma appears to be important as well. Children who have to deal with neglect or abuse in their formative years are especially vulnerable to mental health problems and may well develop BPD if they don't get the help and emotional support they need for normal social development.

Brain imaging research looking at people with BPD suggests that self-harm plays an important role in reducing stress and helping to regulate emotions. One recent study comparing BPD and non-BPD adults in terms of how they responded to stress showed that an incision in the forearm not only led to reduced stress for BPD adults but also showed reduced activity in regions of the brain linked to stress, including the amygdala and limbic system.

While many people with BPD report feeling relief and increased emotional control after harming themselves, there can be other motives as well. This can include a deep-seated need for self-punishment as well as a form of sensation seeking.

While BPD remains the most common personality-disorder diagnosis linked to self-harm, other personality disorders have been identified as well. For example, avoidant personality disorder (also known as anxious personality disorder or APD) is a diagnosis often given to people reporting strong feelings of inadequacy, social anxiety, a fear of being judged by others, and avoidance of social interaction despite wanting to be close to others. While people with APD may also self-harm as a way of reducing tension, they are more likely to use it to cope with being rejected or abandoned.

Even though BPD and APD have traditionally been considered hard to treat, some of the newer therapies have had good success in helping to control personality disorder symptoms and improve overall quality of life. On the other hand, people with personality disorders who *don't* seek treatment rarely get better on their own and often develop more serious mental health problems later in life.

Some psychotherapies proven to be especially helpful in treating BPD and other personality disorders include:

- Cognitive behavioral therapy (CBT)—By helping people with personality disorders change their underlying core beliefs about themselves and the people around them, CBT can reduce the emotional and behavioral problems often associated with BPD and APD. This can also include self-harm and suicidal thinking.

- Dialectical behavior therapy (DBT)—Focusing on mindfulness, or basic awareness of one's own emotions and how they can affect behavior, DBT can be used to control self-destructive behavior and improve social relationships. DBT also deals with the dialectical tension between our need for acceptance and the need for change.

- Schema-focused therapy—Combining CBT with other forms of psychotherapy, this therapy helps people with BPD symptoms overcome the poor self-image that often lies at the root of their personality disorder. By overcoming low self-esteem and developing a stronger self-image, people with BPD can learn how to interact with people around them in a more positive way.

These different treatment programs can be carried out through individual psychotherapy sessions or in the form of treatment groups that can allow patients dealing with personality disorder symptoms and self-harm to discuss their problems with others reporting similar issues. Though not every community will have treatment programs aimed at helping people dealing with personality disorder symptoms as well as self-harm, a family doctor or local mental health organizations can usually refer people in need to a qualified professional with the necessary experience.

18. Is self-harming linked to autism?

Autism is usually defined as a mental condition characterized by difficulty in communicating and forming relationships with other people and in using language and abstract concepts. While the most extreme forms of autism are typically diagnosed in early childhood, autistic symptoms fall on a wide spectrum ranging from severe to relatively mild.

Until recently, there was another term, "Asperger's syndrome," which was used to describe people who have significant autistic symptoms but who are still able to function socially to some extent. This diagnosis has been dropped from the *DSM* and is now considered part of the autism spectrum (the term "autism spectrum disorder" or ASD is also often used).

Though it is still unclear what causes ASD, many of the reported symptoms, including impulsive behavior, hyperactivity, difficulty understanding the feelings of other people, problems with nonverbal communication, and poor social functioning, remain difficult to treat. Many people with ASD symptoms can engage in "rocking behavior" whenever they are feeling frustrated and can often become upset at significant changes to their daily routine. Another common problem often seen in ASD patients is self-harming behavior, which can begin in early childhood and persist right into adulthood.

Some people with autism may even go so far as to deliberately restrain themselves to avoid serious self-injury. This can range from wrapping their arms in towels or heavy clothing to otherwise restricting their hands to keep the self-harm from happening. In extreme cases, this self-restraint can be so severe that their arms and legs can atrophy due to lack of use.

While there is no known cure for autism, symptoms can still be successfully managed with proper treatment. Behavioral therapy and special education can also be effective in helping people with autism overcome self-harming behavior and develop better ways of coping with frustration.

19. Is self-harm linked to childhood sexual abuse?

Research has consistently shown that childhood maltreatment (e.g., physical, sexual, or emotional abuse) can be linked to many different mental and physical health issues. Children who are chronically maltreated often develop problems regulating emotions and controlling their impulses. This can also make them more likely to experience later issues such as depression, anxiety, aggression, substance abuse, and increased risk of suicide. While extensive research has been carried out on how self-harm is linked to childhood sexual abuse, studies looking at other forms of abuse remain relatively scarce. For this reason, it is important to recognize that all forms of early abuse may lead to greater risk of self-harm.

One specific form of abuse that appears significantly linked to later self-harming behavior is referred to as "high-betrayal sexual abuse," that is, sexual abuse from a trusted adult such as a parent, close family member, or caregiver. The emotional trauma associated with abuse from a supposedly trusted adult can be particularly devastating for children, even more so than the abuse itself in many cases. Along with the violation of trust that comes with the abuse, there is often the element of secrecy as well since the abusing adult often resorts to pleading or threats to prevent the child from telling anyone else what is happening. This means that children are forced into the position of concealing their abuse out of fear that they wouldn't be believed or would be blamed for encouraging the abuse in the first place. Even when they find the courage to say what has been happening to them, the trauma of dealing with the criminal justice system can often be as traumatic as the abuse itself.

For young people dealing with this high-betrayal abuse, the likelihood of later suicidal and self-harm behavior seems directly linked to *how long* the abuse has been going on, how close they were to the abuser, and how *early* the childhood abuse began. For incest survivors in particular, the percentage who go on to self-harm can range from 17 to 38 percent according to different studies.

Regardless of the kind of early trauma experienced, self-harm is often linked to negative emotions such as depression, anxiety, and anger as well as poor self-image, feelings of hopelessness, and a general sense of personal worthlessness. By turning these thoughts and feelings inward, self-harmers often find that hurting themselves is the most effective way to help them cope with their lives and keep their inner turmoil under control.

Still, while survivors of childhood sexual and physical abuse are especially prone to self-harm attempts, the reasons they give for these attempts can vary widely. Also, while many people may view self-harm as dangerous and a sign of poor mental health, self-harmers themselves may well regard it as the only way to cope with what is happening to them. Relying on self-harm may often help them overcome feelings of depression and loneliness that might lead to more severe consequences such as substance abuse or suicide.

For survivors of childhood sexual abuse, self-harming may well be considered a sign of resilience since it allows people in pain to take control of their lives until they are able to find a better way to handle what they are thinking or feeling.

20. Is self-harm linked to poor parenting?

Though there have been a number of studies suggesting that self-harmers are more likely to report having a poor relationship with their parents, this isn't always the case.

Certainly the kind of parenting children receive during the first few years of their lives can be critical in terms of whether they develop emotional problems later in life. Children who get a good start with caring parents and a positive early childhood typically develop the cognitive tools they will need later for positive social development. Even if abuse occurs later in their childhood, these children are often better able to recover and move on with their lives.

On the other hand, children who fail to develop a strong emotional bond with a parent or caregiver often have great difficulty socializing with other children as they grow older. In extreme cases, this can lead to developing a personality disorder or acute social phobia. They also become more vulnerable to the kind of damage that childhood abuse can bring, and they are also more likely to turn to self-injury as a way of coping with their emotions.

According to a recent study looking at self-harm in university students, participants reporting a negative relationship with their parents are more likely to engage in severe self-harm and also more likely to report harming themselves to control their emotions. In contrast, participants reporting having a positive relationship with one or both parents might still engage in self-harm, but, overall, their emotional problems and the frequency of their self-harming are usually less severe.

While having a strong relationship with one or both parents can help protect against many of the emotional difficulties usually associated with self-harm, new problems can arise as adolescents grow older and take on the challenges of becoming adults. This is something we all go through as we grow apart from our parents while forming new friendships and new romantic relationships and pass through puberty and beyond.

During this critical stage, young people often become vulnerable to new pressures and temptations that they may feel uncomfortable sharing with their parents and, almost inevitably, develop secrets they prefer their parents not know about. This is especially true for young people coming to terms with homosexuality, substance abuse, promiscuity, and various other issues that make them feel especially isolated since they can no longer turn to their parents for comfort or advice.

It is likely no coincidence that this same period of late adolescence and early adulthood is also when the first signs of mental health problems can first develop, including depression, social anxiety, and suicidal thoughts. Self-harming behavior is also likely to begin and often becomes yet another secret that young people feel the need to keep hidden from their parents.

As parents discover that their children are harming themselves, they tend to go through a period of self-reproach at missing signs that, in hindsight, seemed obvious. Though they may wonder if their own parenting might be to blame for what is happening to their children, this is often not the case.

Whatever the reason for the self-harming, good parental support can be critical for young people in need. For this reason, many young people soon discover that the first step to getting help is opening up to their parents and forming a therapeutic alliance that can see them through the treatment process that follows.

21. Is self-harm linked to eating disorders?

According to the *DSM-5*, eating disorders are serious disturbances in eating behavior such as extreme and unhealthy refusal to eat or overeating, often due to emotional distress or obsessive thoughts about physical appearance or body weight. The most common eating disorders are anorexia nervosa (refusing to eat), bulimia nervosa (extreme overeating followed by purging), and binge eating disorder (eating to deal with distress). Believed to affect about 25 million Americans alone (75% of whom are female), eating disorders are also linked to mental health issues such as depression, social anxiety, and early childhood trauma.

In recent years, research has also shown a strong link between different types of eating disorders and self-harming behavior. According to one new study, the lifetime prevalence of eating disorders in people who self-harm is 27.3 percent overall (21.8% for anorexia and 32.7% for bulimia). Some studies put the percentage of self-harmers who also have eating disorders much higher. Overall, the likelihood of self-harmers also having eating disorders rises sharply in patients with a history of suicide attempts.

Overall, self-harmers who also have eating disorders tend to be more impulsive, are more likely to be substance abusers, and tend to be younger than self-harmers without eating disorders. Gender doesn't seem to be a major factor, however; even though most people suffering from eating disorders are female.

When it comes to personality traits and self-harming in people with eating disorders, one particular trait that researchers have identified is referred to as "harm avoidance." People scoring high in measures of harm avoidance are prone to excessive worrying, shyness, fear of uncertainty, self-doubt, and pessimism. Brain research looking at harm avoidance has linked it to reduced gray matter in key regions of the brain and may be linked to early childhood trauma. Studies have shown that people reporting both eating disorders and self-harm often tend to be high in harm avoidance and impulsive behavior.

Psychiatric studies examining what motivates patients to harm themselves have also turned up some interesting conclusions. Based on structured interviews with anorexia patients, they report being most likely to injure themselves as a way of dealing with the stress of being *forced* to eat. Also, people with eating disorders may often resort to self-harm as a way of regaining control over their bodies, especially their eating patterns. It can also be used as a form of punishment due to feelings of shame over being unable to lose weight.

While most treatment programs currently available tend to deal with self-harm and eating disorders separately, the growing number of patients dealing with both has led to more programs where patients can learn to cope with multiple issues. CBT appears to be especially effective in helping patients identify and modify negative, automatic thoughts and develop healthier coping strategies.

For people experiencing eating disorders and who harm themselves who *don't* seek treatment, the outcome is often grim. Not only can chronic eating disorders lead to severe health problems, but the risk of early death is far higher as well. Admitting to having a problem and asking for help are often the initial steps to a longer life.

22. Can poor sleep increase the risk of self-harm?

Everybody enjoys a good night's sleep. While there are different theories about why the need for sleep first evolved, it seems essential for purging the brain of its toxins and helping the body regenerate, and it even plays a role in how the brain encodes new memories.

Researchers have long recognized that sleep occurs in different stages each night, ranging from more restful sleep with little physical movement to more active phases of sleep during which we experience rapid eye movement and dreaming. These stages seem to be regulated by regions of the brain that also regulate how we respond to day/night cycles as well as control daily body rhythms such as changes in body temperature, mental functioning, and biochemistry.

For people who *don't* get the recommended amount of sleep (typically seven to nine hours each night), the consequences can be severe. Though we all suffer from the occasional bout of insomnia, research looking at chronic sleep deprivation has shown that lack of sleep can lead to impaired judgment, loss of emotional control, reduced mental flexibility, and (at least in some cases) psychotic symptoms. With an estimated 33 percent of Americans reporting loss of sleep for various reasons, it's hardly surprising that investigators often find sleep loss to be one of the main factors in countless industrial and automobile accidents. For people in high-stress jobs, including surgeons, soldiers, and emergency crews, loss of sleep can often lead to serious errors in judgement and potential loss of life.

And sleep is even more important for developing brains. Newborn babies can sleep for 18 hours a day, while youngsters in their first two decades of life often need 10–12 hours of sleep a night. This is likely due to the importance of sleep in shaping neural pathways, which are still forming in young brains.

Several recent studies have also shown that poor sleep is strongly linked to self-harm attempts in young people, even when other mental health factors are taken into account. In a 2016 study looking at more than 2,000 high school students in China, adolescents who harm themselves also reported averaging less than six hours a night of sleep along with frequent nightmares, daytime sleepiness, and poor sleep quality. Another recent study looking at more than 4,000 Korean middle and high school students showed that young people who lost sleep during the week and only engaged in "catch-up sleep" on the weekends were at risk for suicide and self-harm along with mental health problems such as depression.

Though the link between poor sleep quality and self-harm is still being explored by researchers, the information gained so far suggests that symptoms such as daytime sleepiness can be important warning signs that parents and teachers should watch for, especially in young people. Screening for sleep problems in children and adolescents can help identify young people who may be at risk for developing more serious problems such as suicidal thoughts and self-harm behavior. In many cases, poor sleep may often be one of the only real indications that someone is experiencing problems with depression or other emotional issues, which might otherwise be well hidden. Encouraging children and adolescents to get the sleep they need can also help reduce the stress they face on a daily basis and make coping that much easier.

23. Can self-harm be linked to brain disorders?

While many patients diagnosed with a wide range of psychiatric and neurological conditions show a high risk of harming themselves, there is still no clear way of telling why this happens.

Researchers have shown that self-harming behavior can occur in many different conditions such as autism, mental retardation, certain forms of epilepsy, and Tourette's syndrome, though the kind of self-harming attempts that occur can be very different. Head-banging, for example, is often seen in children and adolescents who are inpatients in long-term care facilities, but this seems to be more like a compulsion rather than a way of diffusing tension.

Other forms of self-harm behavior such as trichotillomania (compulsive hair-pulling), onychophagia (nail-biting), and face-slapping can also occur, though again this basically seems to be due to compulsive behavior in the patient instead of more well-known forms of self-harming. There is also a rare genetic disorder known as Lesch-Nyhan syndrome in which victims are prone to involuntary muscle jerking along with frequent nail-biting and head-banging.

Another common finding in neurological patients who harm themselves is that they usually also experience related neurological problems such as movement disorders. This can include facial tics, lip-smacking behavior, rocking behavior, parkinsonian symptoms (similar to what is seen in patients with Parkinson's disease), and general movement difficulties. While some of these patients can have normal intelligence, they often show significant cognitive problems, which make it difficult for them to function in regular society.

Advances in neurological research have provided new ways of exploring what is happening in the brains of people dealing with depression and other mental health problems, especially when self-harm is involved. In one recent study comparing the brains of adolescents dealing with depression and self-harm to healthy adolescents, researchers found that depressed adolescents who self-harmed and who were also dealing with social rejection showed significant brain differences. This included greater activation of the medial and ventrolateral prefrontal cortexes and suggested that self-harmers dealing with depression process information about social rejection differently than young people without emotional problems.

There are also significant differences in those regions of the brain linked to pain and reward. As we have seen in Questions 5 and 11, self-harm appears strongly linked to both pain relief and addiction, with brain research suggesting that people who self-harm show greater activity in the thalamus, dorsal striatum, and anterior precuneus, all of which have already been implicated in studies looking at addiction and the perception of pain and pleasure.

One important clue to the possible role of brain impairment in self-harm behavior comes from animal research. While self-harming behavior in nonhuman species such as primates and some species of rodents tends to be relatively rare, it does occur. According to animal researchers at the Tulane National Primate Research Center, about 5 percent of macaque monkey kept in cages with no contact with others of their species will develop different kinds of self-harm behavior such as self-biting. Certain medications such as naltrexone can reduce self-harm behavior, while brain studies show that unmedicated self-harmers have significant brain differences, including greater atrophy in white and gray matter.

Though this kind of research is still relatively new, insights from neuroscience may provide clues to better treatments for a wide range of mental health problems as well as more effective help for people who self-harm.

24. What is alexithymia, and how is it linked to self-harming?

Alexithymia is a personality trait characterized by inability to identify feelings or emotions as well as being unable to recognize emotions in others. First identified in 1973 by psychologist Peter Sifneos, the term literally means "no words for mood" in classical Greek. People high in alexithymia often have extreme difficulty forming social attachments or appreciating how other people are feeling. While not considered a mental health disorder in itself, alexithymia is often confused with borderline and antisocial personality disorder, though they are very different.

Though only occurring in 10 percent or so of the general population, people with alexithymia are often at risk for many other mental health disorders, including ASD and posttraumatic stress disorder. In fact, one study found that 41 percent of Vietnam veterans dealing with posttraumatic stress also experience alexithymia, while other studies found similar results in Holocaust survivors and victims of domestic violence.

Studies have also shown that alexithymia can be a significant predictor of self-harm behavior, particularly in young people with a history of abuse and traumatic symptoms such as dissociation. Though the link between alexithymia and self-harm seems stronger in women than men, it does suggest that being unable to recognize emotion may make young people more vulnerable to both self-harm and suicidal behavior.

People with alexithymia also score poorly on measures of emotional intelligence (EI), which is often defined as the capacity to recognize your own emotions and the emotions of other people. It also refers to our ability to manage our own emotions and to use our awareness of emotions to guide thinking and behavior. EI became a popular topic following the 1995 release of a best-selling book by psychologist Daniel Goleman. Though still controversial, studies looking at EI have shown a strong link with mental health, job performance, and leadership skills.

Not surprisingly, people who self-harm often report difficulties controlling their emotions and are also prone to depression and social anxiety. Another interesting finding deals with how well self-harmers are able to recognize emotions in other people. Being able to recognize emotions based on facial expressions is an important part of having a successful social life, and adolescents who either attempt suicide or engage in self-harm seem to be significant problems with reading facial expressions. One example of this can be seen in a 2016 study comparing adolescents who have attempted suicide, self-harming adolescents, and adolescents without mental health problems. When shown a series of child and adult faces with a range of different emotions, the suicidal and self-harm groups showed significant problems recognizing negative expressions, particularly sadness and fear.

While different theories have been proposed for what can cause these kinds of emotional problems and how they can lead to self-harm behavior, no clear answer has been found to date. Still, mental health professionals working with young people who harm themselves often find that helping them learn to find more constructive ways to express their emotion can be an important part of overcoming self-harm and many of the other mental health issues they may be experiencing.

25. Are self-harmers more impulsive?

Impulsivity or impulsiveness is usually defined as the tendency to act on impulse without any prior planning or thought. Whether it involves blurting out something inappropriate without thinking about how people might react, doing something risky without considering the consequences, or attacking someone who says or does something upsetting, impulsivity is a common symptom in many disorders. These include antisocial and borderline personality disorder, bipolar disorder, attention-deficit hyperactivity disorder (ADHD), and certain kinds of brain damage.

Researchers looking at impulsivity have identified two main components: acting without proper planning or thought and choosing short-term goals over long-term ones. While impulsivity isn't always a bad thing, especially for those who choose to be spontaneous or unconventional, people high in impulsivity often experience problems with how they relate to others and their proneness to risky behaviors such as suicidal behavior and self-harm attempts.

Though self-harm can have numerous causes, studies have consistently shown that habitual self-harmers often have difficulty recognizing the consequences of their actions (non-planning impulsiveness). In fact, researchers have shown that many self-harmers spend less than five minutes considering harming themselves before acting on that impulse. Self-harmers are also more likely to engage in other forms of impulsive behavior such as substance abuse, impulse buying, binge eating, and gambling.

Part of the problem of examining the link between impulsivity and self-harm is that impulsivity can often mean different things depending on how it's measured by researchers. Not only can impulsivity be considered a personality trait that everyone has to some extent and which can be measured by psychometric tests, but it can also occur as the kind of impulsive behavior seen in people with psychiatric and neurological problems. One prominent model suggests that there are different types of impulsivity, including mood-based impulsivity (rash or impulsive behavior in response to negative emotions such as sadness or anxiety), sensation seeking (a preference for new or risky experiences), lack of perseverance (abandoning attempts to reach goals), and lack of premeditation (acting rashly without considering the consequences). These different dimensions can explain why research studies looking at self-harm don't always find clear evidence that impulsivity is a factor.

Some researchers argue that there are different pathways to impulsive behavior, which can lead to people harming themselves. Recently, a team of researchers examined 28 studies exploring different kinds of impulsivity and how they can relate to self-harm. As expected, they found a significant link between impulsivity and self-harm in young people aged 11–25. It played a strong role in deliberate suicide attempts as well.

Looking at different kinds of impulsivity, they found that mood-based impulsivity played a strong role in first-time self-harm attempts. On the other hand, lack of premeditation and lack of perseverance seemed to play a greater role in self-harm attempts that occur due to habit. In other words, while people may *first* harm themselves due to emotional distress or pain, lack of self-control makes them unable to resist the temptation to keep harming themselves. If their first-time experience teaches them that self-harm can be useful in controlling negative emotions, it can become a habit that is hard to break for people with poor self-control.

There are effective treatments available to help control impulsive and self-harm behavior, including medication, behavior modification and CBT, and parent-child interaction therapy. For people with impulse problems who are self-harming, opening up about needing help is a vital first step.

◆◆◆

Culture, Media, and Self-Injury

26. Are self-harm attempts only a problem in the Western, industrialized world?

Until fairly recently, most research studies looking at people who self-harm have been largely limited to North America (particularly the United States and Canada), parts of Europe (especially the United Kingdom), Australia, and New Zealand. As more health professionals become aware of self-harm worldwide, it is now being reported in many other countries, including China, Israel, India, Jordan, Hong Kong, and Turkey. Unfortunately, accurate statistics showing how often self-harm occurs in countries around the world remain scarce despite efforts from global health organizations to help young people who may be at risk no matter where they are.

Part of the problem in determining how common self-harm really is worldwide is the lack of a universally accepted definition of self-harm behavior. While most countries draw a distinction between suicide attempts and nonsuicidal self-injury, many countries do not, and their statistics often differ as a result. Even for countries using similar definitions, the prevalence rate can differ widely depending on whether or not self-harm attempts are being recorded accurately.

According to the results of the recent "Saving and Empowering Young Lives in Europe" study comparing self-harm and suicide attempts among participating European countries (including Israel), the rate of reported self-harm attempts ranged from 10.4 percent in Germany to only 1.9 percent in Romania, though this may be primarily due to differences in available health care and likelihood of seeking medical attention.

Another issue to consider is how different cultures may view self-harm behavior, whether or not suicide was intended. Since many of these same countries often lack adequate mental health services or keep actual statistics about suicide and self-harm, there is no real way to tell how common the problem really is.

As we have seen in Question 6 self-harm has a very old history, and many cultures around the world have examples of behavior that we would label as self-harm, though they are an accepted part of these different cultures. Many of these behaviors are often intended as rituals for healing, religion, or to show membership in a social group. During religious pilgrimages, for example, many Christian or Muslim pilgrims often whip themselves to show their religious devotion or as a way of punishing themselves for sin.

In Hindu cultures, there are also religious ascetics known as sadhus who regularly mutilate themselves to show their devotion. Some even pierce their tongues and cheeks with pins and carry heavy idols from hooks fastened inside their skin. In many Native American Plains cultures, young men can show their courage by completing an eight-day Sun Dance. The dance ends with warriors being suspended from a Sacred Pole while skewers rip through their chest muscles. The point of this ordeal is to have a sacred vision that can guide warriors for the rest of their lives.

Despite these enormous cultural differences in what kind of behaviors can be considered self-harm, it is becoming more widely recognized as a health problem around the world, and, as a result, more people than ever are coming forward and asking for help.

27. Can media stories about self-injury attempts do more harm than good?

Though researchers have identified numerous risk factors linked to self-harming behavior, it is still unclear why self-harm attempts have been rising in recent years and what could be influencing this new epidemic. As we have seen in Question 15, social contagion resulting from seeing friends or acquaintances harm themselves may be one explanation but probably not a complete one. But what about movies and television shows featuring people who self-harm? Or perhaps even candid media interviews from respected stars who admit to having harmed themselves in the past?

For young people, especially those between ages 14 and 30, going to movies remains one of the most popular forms of entertainment available. According to Albert Bandura's social cognitive theory, repeated exposure to movies featuring people engaging in certain kinds of behavior can increase the likelihood of people copying this behavior, especially if they identify strongly with the characters they are seeing. While concern about the message movies can convey has resulted in rating systems to ensure that nonadults don't see material that might be harmful, these rating systems usually focus on sexual themes and ignore other possibly harmful messages.

Research has already shown that movies featuring characters who smoke, drink, or abuse drugs can lead to more positive attitudes about these behaviors and may also make viewers more likely to imitate them— all of which definitely raises concerns about how self-injury is often portrayed in the media.

Until recently, movies and television shows featuring self-harmers were fairly rare, and, if shown at all, it was usually as a sign of mental illness or suicidal thinking. But media examples of self-injury are becoming much more common. One 2009 study examining self-injury in movies found 23 examples of self-injury in movies released between 2001 and 2005 alone (and likely even higher now). This was in sharp contrast to the three examples found in movies released between 1966 and 1980. That same study found a similar increase in music lyrics about self-harm, with 38 songs released between 2001 and 2005 referring to self-harm versus only one example of a self-harm song released before 1985.

While this greater exposure to self-harm in media can have a positive benefit in helping self-harmers feel less isolated, many researchers are worried about how self-injury is often portrayed. Fictional characters who harm themselves are rarely shown to need treatment or to experience any kind of long-term consequences from their actions. Not only does this make self-harm seem glamorous, but many of these movies and television shows can also spread dangerous misinformation.

Among the television shows that have featured characters harming themselves are *House M.D.*, *Degrassi*, *Seventh Heaven*, *Grey's Anatomy*, *Will and Grace*, and *Nip/Tuck*. The 2004 film *Thirteen* featured a photogenic teenager, Tracy, whose addiction to self-harm resembles drug abuse in many ways. Though some producers have attempted to make the self-harming behavior as realistic as possible, most of the self-harming fictional characters seen in movies make it seem less dangerous than it really is.

A 2013 study provided the best evidence to date that films featuring characters who harm themselves can influence attitudes about self-harm as well as self-harm behavior. The study interviewed over 300 individuals ranging in age from 18 to 30 about whether they had seen any of the 30 films identified by researchers as featuring self-harm. These included films such as *Black Swan, Thirteen, Gothika, A Beautiful Mind, Fight Club,* and *The Da Vinci Code.* The study participants were also questioned about their knowledge about self-harm behavior as well as whether they had ever harmed themselves.

Results showed that seeing these films helped shape attitudes about self-harm and, in many cases, influenced viewers to copy what they saw on the screen. The likelihood of copycat behavior seemed greatest when viewers identified with characters in the film, especially when the characters were sympathetic and likable. In the same way that movies about suicide can often influence suicidal behavior in vulnerable film viewers, making viewers more aware of self-harm can often backfire.

To help counterbalance the way self-harm is often presented, numerous real-life celebrities have also come forward with their own stories. As you can see in the Introduction, stars such as Johnny Depp, Angelina Jolie, and Christina Ricci have been candid about their experiences and the long-term consequences of their self-harming. Unfortunately, many of these media interviews tend not to dwell on the negative aspects of self-harm and often make it seem glamorous and even romantic. Media stories about self-harm can also lead to copycat behavior in much the same way that celebrity suicides do.

Recognizing the potential dangers of copycat behavior and popular media, many organizations, including the American Association of Pediatrics and the Center for Media Literacy, are pushing for more education to teach young people to question what they are seeing or hearing. Along with encouraging parents to be more vigilant about the kind of programs their children are watching, educational techniques have been developed to help students become more aware of how media can influence the way they behave. These techniques can also be used to boost awareness about self-harm and to encourage self-harmers to seek the help they need.

And then there is the Internet that has created entire online communities allowing self-harmers to communicate with one another in ways they never could before. More of this will be discussed in the next section.

28. Is there an online self-harm subculture?

With the rise of the Internet, the opportunities for sharing ideas with people from other parts of the world seem greater than ever. Certainly we are seeing more websites, bulletin boards, social networking groups, and video links dedicated to self-harm topics than ever before. While many of these online groups are intended to allow self-harmers to share their stories in a nonjudgmental and accepting way, there are risks as well for young people contemplating self-harm for the first time.

Although many self-harm support groups have established websites for spreading useful information to people in need (some of these sites are listed in the Directory of Resources), there are other websites that send a very different message. By sharing graphic images, videos providing a "how-to" guide to self-harm, and suggestions about the different ways self-harm can be used to cope with stress or isolation, vulnerable people can gain new ideas for ways to harm themselves as well as further trigger self-harm episodes. Also, since these sites allow self-harmers to become part of a larger online community, they may be more reluctant to seek outside help if they feel all their needs are being filled online.

A 2005 study identified over 500 self-harm Internet message boards (and the number is almost certainly higher now). Though most of these boards provide support and information, they can also include potentially harmful tips such as how to conceal wounds, sharing new self-harm methods to try, and how to avoid detection for as long as possible.

And there can be more subtle ways for self-harmers to identify one another online. A recent study looking at Instagram and other social media sites where users can exchange messages, images, and videos identified certain *hashtags* that are popular in the self-harm community. Hashtags are words or terms preceded by a # symbol and can be used in search engines to find specific topics. Though Instagram is supposed to issue a content advisory for any photo or hashtag linked to potentially harmful material, changing the spelling or using more subtle terms can often bypass this.

Among the more popular self-harm community hashtags (at least for now) are #selfharmmm, #selfinjuryy, #blithe, and #cat. There is even a #MySecretFamily hashtag identifying a broader community of self-harmers and others experiencing mental illness. According to the study, there were nearly 2 million #MySecretFamily Instagram posts, and its popularity is growing.

Certainly the kind of online content being produced that features self-harm topics shows an enormous burst of creativity. Photographs, digital videos, poems, blog posts, and drawings all demonstrate the need for many self-harmers to reflect on their experiences and to share them with others. Interviews with some of the contributors suggest that creating and sharing this content can become a coping strategy in its own right. Still, despite the popularity of this kind of content, researchers remain divided over whether online sharing can act as a trigger for self-harm behavior or help prevent it. Both are likely true.

As the online self-harm community continues to grow, researchers, parents, and health care professionals are raising serious concerns about the kind of impact this new online content is having on potential self-harmers. While helping vulnerable young people feel less isolated is certainly important, the potential link between the rise in online self-harm content and the rising number of self-harm attempts being reported worldwide is something that should be taken seriously.

29. Is body piercing linked to self-harm?

In recent years, we have been seeing a sharp rise in different kinds of body modification practices, often intended to make people look more attractive, to show membership in particular social groups, or simply to imitate actors, athletes, or rock stars who show off their own piercings and tattoos.

Along with more familiar forms of body modifying, new accessories such as nose rings, tattooing, unusual hair styles, and even extensive facial alterations carried out by willing surgeons seem to be entering the mainstream. In fact, many people are taking body modification to extreme lengths and developing new fads such as "pearling" (genital beading), scrotal implants, teeth blackening, eyeball tattooing, implanting jewelry in the outer layers of the eye, tongue cutting, and so forth.

Not that there is necessarily anything new about body modification. As psychiatrist Armando Favazza pointed out in his classic 1996 book, *Bodies under Siege*, body modification is as old as history itself, with many cultures advocating extensive mutilations that might seem impossible to understand from our own perspective. Examples such as *ta moko* in Maori culture and even many healing rituals found in shaman traditions from around the world can seem bizarre and even horrifying, but they are still being widely practiced.

It was Favazza who suggested that the rising popularity of body modification may also be strongly associated with self-harm behavior. Looking at 173 students who had attended an accredited school where they could learn body piercing, Favazza found that 58 percent had a history of self-cutting. Though there is little research examining body modification practices and how it might relate to self-harm, those few studies that do exist seem to support Favazza's conclusion.

For example, a 2008 study of over 400 individuals who had body piercings and tattoos found that 27 percent admitted to having a history of self-cutting That same study also showed that body piercings, tattoos, and other forms of body modifications seem to act as a form of therapy with many former self-harmers engaging in body modification to control the impulses that might otherwise lead them to harm themselves.

As Favazza further points out, the rising popularity of body modification may be contributing to the increased number of self-harm cases being reported in many countries. He suggests that the pain associated with body piercing and tattooing may lower the fear threshold associated with self-injury. Becoming more desensitized to pain makes it easier to engage in different forms of self-harm (or at least more willing to think about it).

Tattoos and other forms of body modification are also becoming extremely popular among prisoners, especially in young offenders. In fact, research has shown that the number of tattoos of a young offender is highly correlated with aggressive behavior, fighting, and self-injury. Perhaps it's not that surprising that more young people are adopting tattoos and other body markers in an attempt to appear more "badass."

There is even a new movement known as "urban primitivism" that has gained popularity in recent years. Inspired by a 1989 book, *Modern Primitives*, by Roland Loomis (a.k.a. Fakir Musafar), the urban primitive movement advocates the use of "rite of passage" rituals found in preindustrial cultures to give people a sense of connection to their ancestral beliefs. Much like young Maori rediscovering *ta moko* for the first time, urban primitives engage in body modification such as scarification (etching or branding images or designs in the skin), flesh hook suspending, corset training, body piercing, branding, and tattooing adapted from "primitive" traditional societies. Often intended as a "rite of passage," many engage in this kind of body modification due to spiritual curiosity or as a form of personal growth.

Though people can engage in body modification for various reasons, available evidence does suggest that many self-harmers may find themselves "graduating" to self-modification as a way of taking charge of their bodies. Whether or not this is a positive development will depend on how far they are willing to take it.

30. Why do people in prisons harm themselves?

Self-harm behavior is a major health challenge for the criminal justice system, particularly since self-harmers are most likely to attempt or commit suicide at some point during their sentence. While self-harm can occur at any age, most studies to date have focused on young offenders who are often coping with prison for the first time in their lives and tend to be far more impulsive than more mature inmates.

A recent Australian survey of young offenders found that 21 percent reported thinking about self-harm at some point in their lives while 16 percent actually harmed themselves. As expected, offenders with a history of childhood abuse or psychiatric problems were the most likely to commit suicide or self-harm. Also, though the majority of these attempts are carried out by male prisoners, female prisoners seem especially vulnerable to self-harm.

According to available statistics from the United Kingdom, 26 percent of all incidents of prisoner self-harm were carried out by women prisoners, even though they only represent about 5 percent of the total prison population. This suggests that about one woman in five will either self-harm or attempt suicide while imprisoned, a rate substantially greater than what can be expected for women living in the community.

Another factor that seems to be linked to the risk of self-harm is whether or not offenders have a history of violence. According to recent research, violent offenders are four times more likely to self-harm than nonviolent offenders and are also more likely to experience depression and thoughts of suicide.

And then there are contributing factors related to prison conditions themselves. Prison life can often magnify the kind of problems that can lead to self-harm behavior. This includes the high stress of incarceration, the likelihood of being bullied or assaulted, being isolated from family, the general noise and discomfort of cells, which can lead to loss of sleep, and the mental health problems to which prison inmates are particularly vulnerable such as substance abuse and personality disorder. Some prisoners also have more serious psychiatric and neurological problems such as schizophrenia and brain damage.

As for what might motivate prison inmates to harm themselves, the four-factor model of self-harm discussed in Question 9 can help provide some insight. Much like self-harmers living outside of prison, people who self-harm in prisons often justify their actions as a way of escaping from toxic situations or to force the people around them to take their demands seriously. It can also be used as a way of defusing tension or to cope with emotions. Unfortunately, prison staff may often interpret the self-harm attempt as a trick to getting better treatment while inside and ignore the prisoner's demands, possibly until it's too late.

Even when self-harm attempts are taken seriously, there are usually limits to what can be done to help prisoners cope with prison life. Group treatment programs available for prisoners usually focus on issues such as substance abuse or whether or not they will reoffend. While individual counseling is also available, there tend not to be enough counselors to go around, and weekly sessions may not be enough to help prisoners in need. Until better prison treatment programs become available, self-harm will continue to be a fact of life for prisoners.

31. Why are self-harm attempts going unreported in some countries?

As we have seen in Question 26, there is no one universally accepted definition of self-harm behavior. In fact, practices such as cutting and self-mutilation may have entirely different meanings across many different cultures. Even in Western countries, health statistics can be confusing since many of these countries often don't make a distinction between suicide attempts and nonsuicidal self-injury. Not only does this make a difference in terms of how health statistics are reported but also how self-harmers may be treated.

Until fairly recently, suicide was illegal in virtually every country around the world, including the United States. In the United Kingdom and other British territories, the penalty for suicide often involved what was known as an *ignominious burial*. This called for the body to be buried at a crossroads with a stake driven through the heart. Any property belonging to the suicide was also seized by the Crown, and family members were completely disinherited. It wasn't until the mid-19th century that these laws were abolished. Even people *attempting* suicide were either imprisoned or locked up in asylums, possibly for the rest of their lives.

While the laws surrounding suicide (and self-injury) have changed in most places, many countries around the world still make suicide a criminal offense punishable by lengthy prison sentences. As you might expect, self-harmers in those countries are often reluctant to ask for help out of fear that they could be arrested instead.

Countries that are known to jail people who attempt suicide include Ghana, Kenya, Uganda, Tanzania, Sudan, Brunei, Bangladesh, the Bahamas, India, Singapore, Jordan, Malaysia, Pakistan, Saudi Arabia, Yemen, and Papua New Guinea. In North Korea, interestingly enough, while attempting suicide isn't illegal, family members can be arrested for not stopping it. For many other countries, actual information on how suicide can be treated by the courts isn't available.

Even in countries without clear laws against suicide, the stigma surrounding suicide and other mental health problems is extremely strong. Many religions also have extremely strong restrictions against suicide and often deny families the right to a proper religious burial unless they can produce a medical certificate proving that their relative was insane at the time of death.

For these reasons, families often conceal suicides whenever possible to avoid embarrassment or shame. When deaths do occur, they tend to either bury the body privately or pretend that the death was accidental. Though self-harmers prefer to conceal what they are doing from their family, the stigma against suicide typically gives them an added incentive not to admit what is happening. It also means that they often feel more isolated than ever adding to the emotional burden they are carrying.

Though media stories about self-harm are helping to break through the barriers faced by vulnerable people in many societies, we will probably be dealing with the stigma surrounding suicidal and self-harm behavior for a long time to come. This means that health care workers around the world need to be more aware than ever about how cultural barriers can prevent people from seeking out the help they need.

32. Are sexual minorities more vulnerable to self-harm attempts?

Coming out as gay, lesbian, or transgender can be scary at any age, but adolescents and young adults trying to come to terms with their same-sex attractions can be especially vulnerable to the emotional problems leading to self-injury. Not only does belonging to a sexual minority often mean feelings of isolation and fear of being discovered but problems with poor self-esteem and depression as well.

As you might expect, research studies have consistently showed that sexual minority youth are far more likely to attempt suicide or self-harm than their heterosexual peers. One recent study looking at 19–24-year-old young people in Ireland found that participants in the sexual minority group had a fivefold increased risk of suicide and a 6.6-fold likelihood of self-harm behavior.

For transgender individuals (especially transgender males), the risk of self-harm and suicide is even greater, even if they are undergoing treatment for gender reassignment. Factors linked to higher self-harm risk in transgender males and females include poor self-esteem, poor social support (particularly from family), and lower satisfaction with their bodies.

But along with the stress of coping with being part of a sexual minority is the very real sense of isolation that comes from being unable to talk to family or friends about what is happening. Given the legal, religious, and cultural barriers that are often in place, this typically means that young people belonging to sexual minorities rarely have the kind of family support that their heterosexual peers often take for granted. And when resorting to self-harm to manage stress, the fear associated with coming out can also make it harder to ask for help, especially in places that make homosexuality a criminal offense.

Other factors that can lead to sexual minority individuals becoming more likely to self-harm are being bullied and *internalized homophobia*. This refers to the self-loathing that many sexual minority individuals experience when they internalize the harmful messages they hear about being homosexual or transgender. Believing that they are inferior or damaged because they aren't part of the heterosexual majority can lead to emotional distress and a need to punish themselves, whether through self-harming or suicide attempts.

In looking at the link between bullying and self-harm, a recent study of 1,870 adolescent Irish males found that the risk of lifetime self-harm was four times greater for victims of bullying than for nonvictims. Since taunts about sexual orientation are common with bullies, sexual minority adolescents are especially prone to the emotional distress often experienced when in the closet.

Though greater acceptance and becoming part of a larger network of sexual minority individuals can help with the feelings of isolation and self-loathing, the coming out process can be long and painful. But it is also necessary. While self-harm behavior might help with the process of coping with short-term stress and mental pain, it is only through coming out to friends and family as well as being willing to ask for treatment that real healing can begin.

33. Are military veterans coping with trauma more likely to harm themselves?

Suicide among returning military veterans and soldiers stationed far from home has always been disturbingly common. Since 2004, however, the number of suicides among soldiers actively serving in Iraq and Afghanistan has gained more attention than ever. Even for veterans who have returned home and reentered society, research has suggested that the likelihood of committing suicide is substantially higher than for males and females in the general population.

To help curb suicide among returning veterans, the U.S. Veterans Health Administration (VHA) established the Patient Safety Improvement (PSI) program. The purpose of this program was to identify ways of preventing veterans receiving care from harming themselves. While focusing primarily on suicide, they also looked at different types of self-injury whether suicide was intended or not.

In a 2011 study examining the data collected as part of the PSI program, researchers found that veterans who injured themselves were substantially more likely to be diagnosed with depression or other emotional disorders, substance abuse, and posttraumatic stress disorder (PTSD). Among self-injurers, 32 percent also had a diagnosis of personality disorder. While 80 percent of self-injurers were men, women seemed more likely overall to injure themselves. About 10 percent of the patients in the sample had injured themselves more than once.

When questioned about why they injured themselves, 82.2 percent reported acting on impulse and only about 18 percent admitting that they had planned to harm themselves. Among self-injurers, overdosing was the most common method used with self-cutting being the second most common. Repeat self-injurers were more likely to be women and to be separated from their spouse when their self-injury occurred. Approximately 36 percent made no attempt to seek medical attention after harming themselves.

Overall, what the researchers found was that women and younger veterans were more likely to injure themselves with no intention of committing suicide, and most self-injurers said that there was no previous planning. In fact, half of all self-injurers reported harming themselves within an hour or less of first thinking about it. Veterans who self-harmed as part of a more long-term plan and who didn't act on impulse were also more likely to have intended to die from their injuries.

So, what do these results suggest? According to Joiner's theory about suicide (discussed in previous sections), people who commit suicide usually develop their capability for suicidal behavior from prior exposure to traumatic events in their life. While this can be due to childhood trauma, domestic violence, and so forth, veterans who have served overseas and faced situations in which they were at high risk for violence or death (including seeing it occur to the people around them) do appear to develop an increased capability for suicide and self-harm as a result.

Given the unique stress that veterans often face, even after they return home to civilian life, relying on extreme coping strategies such as self-harm and substance abuse may well help them keep their emotions in check. But it is often not enough to prevent more serious consequences such as suicide, which is where the need for professional help is greatest.

❖

Assessment, Treatment, Prevention, and Life after Self-Injury

34. Should self-harm be classified as a psychiatric disorder?

As we have already seen in Question 1, NSSI is listed in the latest edition of the *Diagnostic and Statistical Manual of Mental Disorders* for possible inclusion as a disorder in future editions. Still, the proposed criteria (also described in Question 1) for this new diagnosis usually only applies to the most extreme cases of self-harm behavior as opposed to more casual self-harmers. But some researchers are debating whether self-harm should be classified as a psychiatric disorder at all.

When self-harm was first identified by mental health professionals, it was treated as being caused by mental illness, usually because the most extreme examples were seen in people suffering from severe psychiatric problems. But as more self-harmers came to tell their own stories about why they were injuring themselves, researchers began to question whether self-harm was a disease in its own right or just a symptom for other problems that needed to be addressed. They also came to recognize that treating self-harm as a mental disorder may very well make the problem worse in many cases.

The decision to begin self-harming can occur for a wide variety of reasons. While many young people may injure themselves as a way of coping with negative emotion or trauma, others may start after hearing about it from friends or acquaintances (not to mention in the popular media). It is often due to the effect of social contagion (see Question 15) that many people may find themselves experimenting with self-harm as a way of imitating others.

There are even entire subcultures dedicated to "emo" (short for emotional) or "goth" that encourage young people to follow certain standards of culture, behavior, and culture. This often includes a preference for emo bands such as Death Cab for Cutie, wearing black wristbands and developing a general appearance of gloominess and depression through the use of self-harm behavior and body piercing (see Question 29). Also, like with many fads, young people who start self-harming because they see it as the "in" thing to do often end up "spinning out" (stopping) once it loses its appeal.

While self-harm can still be potentially life threatening, especially if taken to extremes, most self-harmers rarely reach that stage. In cases of mild self-harming, for example, it may never get past one or two episodes of superficial scratching and a decision to stop after concluding that it isn't working very well as a way of dealing with stress or unpleasant experiences.

Parents and teachers dealing with young people who self-harm need to recognize that this kind of behavior is often the tip of the iceberg. Treating self-harming as a disorder may mean overlooking other mental health issues that may have led the self-harming in the first place. Considering that many self-harmers are already ashamed or afraid of how others will view what they are doing, treating their self-harming behavior as a psychiatric disorder can make them more reluctant than ever to open up and ask for help.

As mental health professionals learn to deal with self-harmers as non-judgmentally as possible, the question of whether it should be treated as a psychiatric disorder is becoming a nonissue.

35. Do self-harm attempts go away over time?

There is no such thing as a typical self-harmer. Self-harming behavior can fall on a wide spectrum depending on the type of method being preferred, how severe the attempts can be, and whether they seek medical attention or ask for any kind of help. For this reason, it can be difficult to make clear conclusions about how frequently self-harm attempts occur and whether these attempts can stop on their own.

According to a 2008 study looking at hospital admissions for self-harm in the United Kingdom, 33 percent of self-harmers who go to hospital seeking treatment will reinjure themselves at some point in the following 12 months. Half of all repeat attempts will occur in the first 3 months after the first attempt, while two-thirds will occur within the first 6 months. In some cases, however, a follow-up self-harm attempt can occur just days after being seen at hospital.

Risk of future self-harming can also depend on the method being used. The highest risk of repeated self-harm attempts occurs in self-cutters or who use more than one method to injure themselves. For people who use more serious methods of self-injury such as deliberate drug overdose or drowning, the risk of repetition is much lower (though the likelihood of accidental death is also much greater).

Factors that can boost the likelihood of future self-harming can include having a history of sexual abuse, drug or alcohol abuse, worrying about sexual orientation, poor self-esteem, social isolation anxiety, or having a family member who is a self-harmer.

There doesn't appear to be a consistent difference in rate of repeated self-harm for males and females, though older adults (35–44 years of age) who are self-cutters show a higher risk of repeated self-harm attempts than younger adults. Also, many self-harmers report dealing with multiple life problems that can lead to feelings of hopelessness. For adolescent and young adult self-harmers, these life problems often focus on difficulties in school or relationships, while for older self-harmers, problems can shift to job worries, relationship issues, or financial difficulties.

Even for repeat self-harmers, there can be important differences. Though many self-harmers often space their attempts over months or longer, hospital emergency departments may find themselves dealing with patients who carry out multiple self-harm attempts within just a few weeks. Researchers have also identified high-volume self-harmers who may have 15 or more emergency department admissions within a four-year period. While only making up less than 1 percent of all self-harmers, these high-volume self-harmers can account for as much as 10 percent of all self-harm attempts treated in hospitals. They also have the highest risk of death, either from deliberate suicide or accidental injury.

As you can see, self-harming is something that needs to be taken seriously, whether it comes to light in a hospital emergency department, in a classroom, or at home. While many people seeing this kind of behavior for the first time may be tempted to do nothing in the hope that self-harmers will simply "grow out of it" in time, the study results shown earlier help demonstrate that self-harming behavior can often become worse if left untreated. This is why getting self-harmers into therapy is so essential, especially in the early stages.

36. What are potential warning signs that parents and teachers should watch for?

Young people can start harming themselves for a wide variety of reasons as you can see from what has been covered in previous sections. All too often, family members and friends are caught by surprise when they discover that young people who appear well adjusted and free of any obvious problems have been harming themselves, sometimes for an extended period of time.

Parents, teachers, and friends need to recognize the different risk factors that might suggest that someone is in a high risk for suicide or self-harm. Though many of these risk factors have already been covered in different sections of this book, here are some of the most common ones:

- Psychiatric or emotional illness (including depression and social anxiety)
- Low self-esteem
- Poor social skills
- Immature or overly rigid coping strategies for dealing with stress
- Impulsive behavior
- Excessive risk-taking behavior (including substance abuse or unsafe sex)
- History of abuse (physical, emotional, or sexual) and/or neglect
- Family history of suicidal or self-harm behavior

While these different risk factors don't necessarily mean that an adolescent or teen will self-harm at some point, they do indicate potential problems that shouldn't be ignored in the hope that they might "grow out of it." At the very least, parents should discuss problems such as these with a family doctor to see if a referral to a mental health professional can be made.

Along with risk factors that suggest the presence of long-term problems that may need professional treatment, there are also specific warning signs for self-harm behavior that parents and teachers need to watch for very carefully. Though self-harmers are often very good at keeping this side of themselves hidden, being alert to these warning signs can make all the difference in terms of early diagnosis and treatment.

Among the most important of these warning signs are:

- frequent cuts, burns, or other injuries, which are either unexplained or for which the excuses given seem very unlikely;

- appearance of cuts or burns, which seem more regular or deliberate than what would be expected of accidental injuries. For example, cuts or burns in a straight line along the arm or back;
- several injuries in the same part of the body, which are at different stages of healing;
- deliberate attempts to keep the injuries hidden such as wearing long-sleeve shirts or jackets despite warm weather;
- a change in the kind of music or style they usually prefer, especially if it involves dark, or emo themes;
- discovering razor blades, knives, or box cutters in their bedroom or some other room in the house that they prefer to use; and
- decline in school performance and the development of mental health symptoms such as depression, social withdrawal, and apathy.

Adolescents and teens who self-harm often carry the instruments they use to cut themselves around in a backpack or purse. Otherwise, they may conceal the objects in their rooms or another part of the house where they are certain they cannot be found. Some of these objects can seem quite innocent and can include safety pins, nail files, box cutters, or a pocket knife. Matches and cigarettes can also be used for self-burning.

Even if a parent or teacher suspects that someone is self-harming, it is still important to be as nonjudgmental as possible in persuading him or her to open up. Not only does this apply to the self-harming but also to the issues that may have led to the self-harming in the first place. Even though this can be especially hard for parents, it is important to avoid emotional confrontations if possible and get the self-harmer to agree to see a professional.

37. How are self-harmers assessed by health professionals?

How self-harmers are assessed by health professionals usually depends on the circumstances under which they are first seen. For many self-harmers, this first assessment often occurs in a hospital emergency department. Even though self-harmers are usually good at concealing what they are doing to themselves, they can still reach the point where their injuries can no longer be hidden.

This is often a key treatment opportunity since, in many cases, it is the first time that self-harmers come forward and ask for help. Though emergency doctors are becoming more aware of self-harm and how they should be treated, their first priority will always be to treat injuries and then take whatever steps are necessary to prevent further injuries while their patients are recovering.

If the self-harmer reported actually intending to commit suicide, then they may be held in an inpatient ward until the suicide risk is reduced. For those self-harmers who are not actively suicidal, however, most emergency departments will refer them to mental health services (provided these services are available in their community) or else notify their family doctor.

When dealing with *repeat* self-harmers, emergency medical professionals will usually treat these cases as being more severe. Though only a small percentage of self-harmers are high-volume cases (usually defined as 15 or more admissions in the previous four years), they can often make up a sizeable percentage of the total number of self-harm attempts dealt with in emergency departments. Repeat self-harmers are treated with particular concern since they are at high risk for suicide, and psychiatric treatment can often be mandatory in such cases.

Despite the growing concern surrounding self-harm attempts and how they should be treated by health professionals, not every hospital will respond in the same way. A recent study in England found that nearly half of all self-harmers leave hospital emergency departments before being properly assessed, whether due to their being impatient over not being treated quickly enough or else out of fear of how staff will react.

To provide a more consistent standard of care, many hospitals have implemented the Manchester Self-harm Rule (MASH) for all cases of deliberate self-harm and attempted suicide. Under this rule, patients are classified as high-risk for repeated self-harm or suicide if they have a previous history of suicide or self-harm attempts, have a history of psychiatric treatment, are receiving current psychiatric treatment, and have a history of benzodiazepine use. While mostly intended to deal with high-risk cases, the MASH rule can help identify self-harmers and allow hospitals to act more effectively.

For most self-harmers, treatment usually occurs through outpatient programs in which self-harmers can either receive one-to-one treatment with a counselor or else take part in a group therapy program for self-harmers. When seeing a therapist for the first time, self-harmers often feel extremely nervous and self-conscious, especially if they are afraid of being thought "crazy" or weird because of what they have been doing (these are the same fears that prevent many self-harmers from seeking treatment in the first place).

Unfortunately, not every mental health professional is going to have experience dealing with self-harmers, and some smaller communities may not have the kind of treatment resources found in larger cities. A competent mental health professional will tell a patient if he or she is better off dealing with someone with more experience and will also make the necessary referral. Self-harmers who discover that a therapist isn't able to provide them with the support they need shouldn't take this as a sign of rejection. Successful treatment usually means finding the best fit between therapists and their patients so that real progress can be made.

38. When is an inpatient program necessary?

While inpatient programs exist for treating self-harmers, this is usually reserved for the cases where there is a strong possibility of suicide. Also, when self-harmers find that they are unable to end their self-harming on their own or with the aid of outpatient therapy, they may consider some of the specialized inpatient programs that are available in many places.

One popular program known as SAFE (Self-Abuse Finally Ends) was founded in 1985 by therapist Karen Contario. The authors of the book *Bodily Self-Harm: The Breakthrough Healing Program for Self-Injurers* Conterio and Wendy Lader, the clinical director for SAFE Alternatives, continue to run the SAFE program at Linden Oak Hospital in Naperville, Illinois, just outside Chicago. The 30-day inpatient program is reserved for patients who specifically request admission and who admit having a problem they can't deal with any other way. Conterio and Lader view this willingness to be admitted as a first step toward successful treatment and say as much in their admission letter.

Once admitted, patients sign a safety contract (see Question 41) stating that they agree not to self-harm during their time inside. As Lader stated in an online interview with WebMD (see the Directory of Resources), "We want to teach them to operate in the real world. That means making choices in response to emotional conflict—healthier choices, rather than just self-injuring to feel better. We want them to understand why they are angry, show them how to handle their anger."

Since inpatients are allowed to shave, they have access to razors and other items that they might potentially use to injure themselves. "They can shave. We don't take belts or shoe laces," Conterio said. "The message we're sending is, 'We believe you're capable of making better choices.'" While inside, self-harmers receive group and individual psychotherapy and are also encouraged to write a journal (see Question 40) to learn how to express their feelings appropriately. If there are other mental health problems, such as depression or anxiety, medication may also be prescribed to help patients function during their 30-day stay.

One of the major treatment goals of the program is to help patients gain self-respect and self-esteem. "Many kids have difficulty dealing with situations and people that make them angry," Lader points out. "They don't have great role models for that. Saying no, standing up to people—they don't really believe they're allowed to do that, especially girls. But if you can't do that, it's very difficult to maneuver the world, survive in the world without someone stronger, more capable than you to fight your battles."

Research looking at how effective the SAFE program can be shows that 75 percent of patients show a decrease in self-injury even two years after participating. "We truly believe that if people can continue to make healthy choices, they won't go back to self-harm," Conterio said. "We get emails that are a blast from the past. Some patients do extremely well. Others regress. Others have finally decided to do the work they learned here. When they apply it, they do well. It all goes back to choice."

While not all inpatient programs have the track record of SAFE, some self-harmers may prefer to go this route if there is an inpatient program available in their area. Ultimately, the decision to enter such a program or relying on outpatient treatment is something only the person seeking treatment can make.

39. What are some of the most common forms of treatment for children and adults who harm themselves?

The causes of self-harming behavior can be extremely hard to pin down, and, for that reason, there is no one-size-fits-all treatment approach for dealing with people who harm themselves. Along with treating the emotional problems that often come with self-injury, there are also the life problems that need to be dealt with. These can include bullying, concerns about sexual orientation, social isolation, relationship problems, and academic concerns—larger issues that self-harmers need to face with the assistance of friends and family and with the guidance of mental health professionals.

At present, research evidence identifies six different forms of psychotherapy that have proven effectiveness in treating self-harmers. These are as follows:

- Dialectical behavior therapy—Known as DBT for short, dialectical behavior therapy is a modified form of cognitive behavior therapy developed in the late 1980s by psychologist Marsha Linehan. Specifically intended for treating BPD cases and people who are chronically suicidal, DBT combines individual and group treatment to help patients identify and reduce self-harming and life-threatening behaviors. Using cognitive techniques, DBT patients are taught how to regulate their emotions, tolerate distress, and practice mindful awareness. Not only have numerous research studies looking at DBT shown positive results in treating self-harmers, but follow-up research also found that benefits can continue long after treatment ends. Unfortunately, most of these studies have focused on adolescent self-harmers, so the benefits of DBT for older adults are not as clear.
- Emotion regulation group therapy—Also referred to as ERGT, this is a specialized form of DBT specifically designed for treating BPD and self-harming. Usually administered in a 14-week group format, ERGT focuses on developing emotional regulation skills and acceptance as well as how to pursue important goals. While not as widely researched as DBT, studies have shown significant reduction in self-harming behavior over a nine-month period following the end of treatment. ERGT was originally intended for use with female patients, and few of the research studies completed to date have looked at how effective it can be with males.
- Manual assisted cognitive therapy—Known as MACT for short, manual assisted cognitive therapy is a six-session focused therapy program designed to help patients understand why they are harming themselves, to relieve distress, and find more constructive ways of coping with their problems. Sessions follow a manual-based approach with units such as "Understanding Self-Harm" and "What to Do in a Crisis." Along with individual therapy, patients rely on bibliotherapy to learn more about self-harming and coping. Though only a few studies have been completed so far, MACT shows promise in reducing self-harm attempts and may be preferable to other approaches since it can be completed in a relatively short time period.
- Voice-movement therapy—Originally developed by therapist Paul Newham, voice-movement therapy (VMT for short) is a form of expressive arts therapy using singing, drama, expressive writing, sound-making, massage, and movement activities to help patients regulate their emotions and increase self-awareness. Again, this is a relatively new treatment approach, and only a few studies have been completed to date that show reasonable effectiveness with self-harmers.

- Dynamic deconstructive psychotherapy and transference focused psychotherapy—The last two treatment approaches, dynamic deconstructive psychotherapy (DDP) and transference focused psychotherapy (TFP), are psychodynamic therapies designed to help self-harmers come to terms with their emotions and improve relationships. Primarily aimed at patients with BPD, early research suggests that DDP and TFP can be effective for self-harmers as well.

No matter which approach is used, the treatment process usually begins with the therapist and the patient getting to know one another and laying the groundwork for a relationship based on trust and mutual respect. A good therapist will also avoid anything that might make the patient uncomfortable or reinforce the feeling of shame or guilt that many self-harmers will have. Once the therapeutic relationship is firmly established, the real treatment can begin.

40. How can self-harmers learn about their triggers?

An essential part of the treatment process involves finding those specific triggers that cause self-harmers to injure themselves. For many self-harmers, this can be an uncomfortable process since it means exploring their thoughts and feelings in a way that they could never bring themselves to do before they entered therapy. One of the first things that many therapists may do with their self-harming patients is to encourage them to start a self-harm diary that records not only when they injure themselves but also the patterns this kind of behavior seems to follow.

For example, do the self-harm attempts occur at a specific time of day or month or possibly according to a self-harmer's menstrual cycle? And do the self-harm attempts occur in a specific room of the house? When are self-harmers most vulnerable to the temptation to injure themselves? What kind of emotional states or problems occur just prior to a self-harm attempt? If self-harming is triggered by anger, writing about this anger as it occurs may be useful instead of waiting until the anger builds up and the self-harming begins.

Creating a self-harm record can serve more than one purpose. Along with learning about what can make self-harmers especially vulnerable to acting out, the very act of writing can help diffuse the crisis and prevent the self-harm impulse from going any further. This record can take the form of a written diary or through audio or video recordings (smartphones can be handy for this).

Though the main purpose of a self-harm record is to help self-harmers identify their own triggers, they can be shared with others as they choose. Reviewing these records with a therapist can help provide a more objective perspective and uncover details that self-harmers may miss.

But it isn't enough to record the self-harm attempts alone. Recording those times when self-harmers felt the urge to injure themselves and successfully resisted that urge can be important as well. Also, recording positive events that make self-harmers feel better about themselves and encourage them to make healthier life choices that might reduce the need to self-harm in future is important.

For self-harmers who feel emotionally numb or have difficulty expressing their own emotions (an especially common problem in trauma victims), this process of recording their emotions can be particularly hard. This is where a therapist can help them explore what feelings and emotions can lead to self-injury and put those feelings into words in a clear manner.

There are risks associated with keeping a self-harm record as well, something that therapists and their patients should discuss beforehand. Some self-harmers may find themselves reliving their emotional tension as they review what they recorded. It can even increase the risk of self-harm at times. This is why therapists and their patients need to go over the self-harm record together so that patients can learn to work through their emotions in a safe environment.

Before beginning a self-harm record, however, it is important that therapists and patients establish a safety contract to reduce the risks associated with self-harm attempts. More of that will be discussed in the next section.

41. What is a safety contract?

Though therapists will attempt to explore the underlying reasons for why their patient is self-harming, that is often a process that may take many sessions. For this reason, the first step when dealing with a self-harming patient often involves establishing a *safety contract* relating to the self-harming behavior. Since most patients aren't going to be able to stop right away, good therapists recognize that demanding can be counterproductive. This is true especially for people who consider their self-harm to be the only coping strategy they know that can actually help them control stress. Being ordered to stop the self-harming right away can lead to them dropping out of treatment altogether.

Safety contracts are similar to the no-suicide contracts that many therapists may use with suicidal patients to prevent them from killing themselves. Although no-suicide contracts tend to be controversial, especially with evidence that are not effective in preventing suicides, safety contracts may be more useful in educating self-harmers about how to avoid serious injury.

In forming a safety contract, therapists encourage patients to be honest and open about their self-harming. That means reporting when it happens and committing themselves to find more constructive coping strategies that might take the place of the cutting or burning.

Even when the self-harming can't be eliminated completely (at least, not right away), patients are usually encouraged to become more aware of *why* they are injuring themselves and what may be triggering this kind of behavior. Patients then become more aware of the different triggers that can lead to self-injury and understand how these triggers formed in the first place. This can be a tricky stage for both the therapist and the patient since many self-harmers are going to feel ashamed or defensive about what they are doing, and opening up to someone else can often make them feel threatened or uncomfortable.

It is at this stage that the therapist needs to remind the patient that he or she is not alone and that self-harm is much more common than most people realize. In establishing a safety contract, therapists and patients basically lay down certain ground rules to prevent more serious problems from developing.

For example, patients who cut themselves can be encouraged to make smaller cuts rather than larger ones or to try scratching themselves rather than using cuts that can break the skin. If they are using a knife or other sharp object, self-harmers can be encouraged to ensure that the instrument they are using is sterile and to follow up the cutting with proper first aid to prevent infection. Self-harmers can also be encouraged to remove razor blades and other sharp objects from where they are living since having these instruments nearby can trigger self-harm behavior.

Therapists can also encourage their self-harming patients to take advantage of their social support networks (friends and family members) who can help them work through their need to injure themselves. This allows them to develop alternative coping strategies that can take the place of the self-harming whenever they encounter their usual triggers.

42. What kind of coping strategies can help with self-harm?

After establishing a safety contract (see previous section), therapists work with their patients to help them overcome the shame and guilt they often experience as well as understand *why* the self-injury is happening. Along with learning to recognize the triggers that can lead to self-harming behavior, therapists can also teach patients different coping strategies that can be used instead of self-injury to deal with stress.

Since not all self-harmers are the same, the kind of triggers that they need to watch for can vary as well. Many self-harmers may have no idea that these triggers exist, and learning about them can provide needed insight into what is happening. Triggers can include anything that makes them feel abandoned or unwanted, such as being rejected by a trusted person, feeling depressed or angry, having an argument, or failing an important test in school. Whatever brings on the sensation of being unwanted or being a failure can be enough to trigger the self-harming.

Therapy also focuses on teaching patients about the nature of stress and healthy ways to keep stress from building up. This includes learning to "listen" to the body and recognizing when anger or anxiety is reaching a danger point. Not surprisingly, many self-harmers may have little experience with positive ways of coping and can benefit from this kind of training.

For people who are prone to self-harming whenever they get angry or frustrated, sublimation toward more constructive activities can be helpful. Instead of punching a wall, they can be taught to punch a pillow or beat a drum, for example. Other activities that can keep the hands busy include writing, drawing, sculpting with clay or Plasticine, crocheting, or ripping paper.

Self-harmers can also be encouraged to remove all potential self-harm aids from their homes. If the self-harm involved cutting with a razor blade, for example, those razor blades could be thrown out or replaced with a safety razor that can't be easily taken apart. This doesn't eliminate the risk of self-harm entirely, but it can make it more difficult by forcing them to find another method that may not be as effective. Also, the time taken to search for a new tool can preoccupy them enough to overcome the impulse to self-harm.

For many self-harmers, it can be extremely valuable to use harmless substitute behaviors that can stimulate the body in ways that resemble pain. These are often referred to as "grounding" strategies since they help detach people from emotional pain and become more centered and focused. For example, plunging the hands into very cold water or rubbing ice cubes on the skin may provide some relief from the tension of wanting to self-harm. Other things to try can include twanging a rubber band on the skin, eating hot peppers, or sniffing a nasal decongestant.

In addition to support from the therapist, self-harmers can also get invaluable help from friends and family members who can provide them with emotional support. Simply being able to talk about what is triggering the self-harm impulse can be enough to deter them from acting out.

Along with the material presented in the treatment sessions, many clinicians will also provide a self-help package that self-harmers can use at home as needed. This package can include a list of coping strategies, telephone numbers of useful resources nearby (including the nearest hospital emergency department), online resources, and audiotapes that can be used as part of homework assignments to help reinforce what is being learned in therapy. People receiving treatment should review the material in this package carefully as another part of the treatment process.

43. What is cognitive restructuring?

In treating different mental health problems, and problem behavior such as self-harming, therapists often focus on the "automatic thoughts" that shape what patients believe about themselves, the people around them, and the world in general. These automatic thoughts are often formed by traumatic early life experiences that can create a distorted view of the world and themselves. For self-harmers, these automatic thoughts can include such beliefs as "I deserve to be punished," "Nobody cares about me," "I am worthless," or "Cutting myself is the only way to take away the pain."

During treatment sessions, the therapist can help patients discover that these automatic thoughts exist, how they came about, and how self-harmers rely on them in making sense of the world. This also means understanding how irrational or exaggerated these automatic thoughts are. Psychiatrist Aaron Beck and his student David Burns identified different *cognitive distortions* that can affect how people can see reality and also help reinforce the negative beliefs associated with depression and other mood problems.

Examples of cognitive distortions include filtering (focusing entirely on negative aspects of a situation while ignoring the positive ones), catastrophizing (always believing the worst case scenario will happen), all-or-none thinking (seeing things in black and white without recognizing that there is a middle ground), or overgeneralization (making broad conclusions based on very limited experience).

Cognitive restructuring involves helping patients recognize the distortions that led to automatic thoughts and learning to overcome these distortions and change their beliefs. During the treatment process, patients learn to challenge these beliefs and identify the cognitive errors they have made. There are a wide range of different possible techniques that can be explored during treatment sessions, and therapists may select the ones that may be most effective for each patient.

With self-harming behavior, patients learn to identify the automatic thoughts that lead to self-harming before challenging and restructuring them. For example, the automatic thought, "I deserve to be punished," can be challenged by exploring how the patient first developed this belief and then recognizing that the patient has done nothing to deserve such treatment. By challenging each automatic thought, patients can reexamine how they are reinforcing the need to harm themselves and replace them with more positive beliefs.

Since self-harming behavior is often linked to other mental health issues such as depression, social anxiety, eating disorders, or hopelessness, exploring and replacing the automatic thoughts that are reinforcing these negative beliefs and behaviors can often help with the self-harming as well.

Cognitive restructuring is just one of the different techniques that therapists may use to help patients understand why they are harming themselves and learn better ways of coping. Still, not every patient will be able to apply cognitive restructuring or the other cognitive techniques right away. For patients feeling overwhelmed by emotional problems such as anxiety or depression, therapists may prefer to focus on teaching emotional coping skills to help patients manage their emotional distress as needed. This is why the treatment process can vary from patient to patient, and, as always, the patient is free to terminate the treatment at any time if he or she does not feel comfortable or doesn't feel ready to explore the problems that underlie self-harming.

44. What is mindfulness therapy?

Mindfulness involves developing an awareness of the thoughts, feelings, and sensations that we experience from one moment to the next. This kind of awareness can be attained through mental training and techniques such as meditation and deep breathing exercises. Originally part of Buddhist and Hindu philosophies, mindfulness has become an important concept in Western medicine in recent years through the work of therapists such as Jon Kabat-Zinn. It was Kabat-Zinn who founded the Mindfulness-Based Stress Reduction program at the University of

Massachusetts in 1979 and showed the benefits of mindfulness therapy in the treatment of a wide range of physical and psychiatric conditions, including depression, stress management, substance abuse, and, more recently, self-harming.

Much like cognitive restructuring, mindfulness techniques such as meditation can be used to halt automatic thoughts by "decentering" all thoughts and feelings that might trigger negative emotions or beliefs. This means learning to stop reacting to these thoughts and simply accepting them without judgment. Patients then realize how automatic thoughts develop and diffuse the impact those thoughts can have.

Also, through exercises intended to make patients more aware of their thoughts and emotions (also known as dispositional mindfulness), they can learn how to regulate their emotions instead of becoming over-whelmed. A related concept is known as "decoupling" since it involves reducing or eliminating the link between inner experiences (e.g., depression or anxiety) and external behaviors (e.g., self-harming).

In addition to helping patients deal with depression, research has shown that different forms of mindfulness therapy can help addicts control their urges and develop their sense of self-control. Programs such as mindfulness-based cognitive therapy have been used in hospitals, clinics, schools, and prisons around the world and appear to be especially useful in preventing relapses for many chronic mental health problems.

Since research has consistently found that people who self-harm generally have difficulty controlling their emotions, researchers are increasingly looking at the role that mindfulness can play in preventing or reducing self-harm attempts. One recent study published in late 2016 found that individuals with a history of self-harm scored significantly lower on mindfulness surveys than non-self-harming individuals. Even when former self-harmers were compared to individuals who were still harming themselves, there was a clear difference in mindfulness scores.

In studies focusing specifically on dispositional mindfulness and how it relates to self-harming behavior, college students scoring high in dispositional mindfulness were also found to be more effective at coping with stress and also had a reduced likelihood of self-harm attempts. Individuals high in mindful awareness also reported a stronger zest for life and, as you might expect, being less likely to self-harm or commit suicide.

While mindfulness therapy is widely used by many treatment professionals helping self-harmers learn emotional control, there are still not that many research studies looking at how effective it can be in curbing self-injury attempts. Early results using treatment programs such as Mindfulness-Based Relapse Prevention (MBRP) are showing a significant drop in self-harm attempts as compared to nontreated self-harmers, though, again, such research is still in the very early stages.

For now, mindfulness therapy is just one of many different therapeutic programs that can be used in treating self-harming behavior and the other emotional problems that often go with it. Though it shows great promise, especially in helping self-harmers learn to regulate their emotions more effectively, more research is needed before mindfulness therapy becomes a common feature in self-harmer programs worldwide.

45. Who should receive group therapy?

Many self-harmers find group therapy to be extremely valuable in helping them come to terms with their self-injuring and what led to it in the first place. Listening to other self-harmers share their own stories can help with the guilt and shame often associated with self-harming as well as make the patients in the group feel less isolated. Also, people in the group can develop deep emotional bonds with other group members and help overcome their own issues in the course of treatment. Still, group therapy isn't for everybody and should be used as part of a broader treatment process along with individual counseling sessions.

Any potential group therapy patient needs to be carefully screened to ensure that he or she benefits from being in a group with other patients. Some patients may not be comfortable sharing their lives with the other group members or may have poor social skills that might lead to them becoming disruptive. Also, socially anxious patients may decide to stay silent without ever participating.

Group therapy patients need to be properly motivated to be part of a treatment group and show proper empathy for what other group members are sharing about their own lives. Most importantly, they need to respect their fellow group members and respect their right to privacy by keeping all information they may learn in the group strictly confidential.

Along with allowing self-harmers who are part of the group to share their stories, group therapy sessions can also include sessions looking at different coping strategies such as relaxation training, social skills development, self-confidence building, anger management, and mindfulness training. Though some self-harmers may not feel that this material is immediately helpful to them, the skills they develop in these sessions can be essential in helping many self-harmers move on with their recovery.

Unfortunately, some group members may feel a need to "compete" with the other patients in the group either through acting as if their problems are more important or else trying to dominate the group and not giving other patients a chance to contribute. Ideally, the ground rules will be laid down at the beginning, and patients may begin with individual counseling until the therapist decides that they are ready to be part of a therapy group.

With self-harmers, there is another issue that needs to be considered. Group members talking about their self-harm behavior may provide graphic details, even if they aren't trying to shock the other people in the group. Hearing many of these details can be deeply disturbing for self-harmers who are dealing with similar issues. This is why therapists need to work with their patients on an individual basis to ensure they are ready to cope with the often intense group therapy sessions that can occur.

By attending group therapy sessions on a regular basis, self-harmers can develop a sense of hope at seeing how other self-harmers have succeeded in overcoming problems very similar to what they are going through. Also, by imitating the examples provided by the therapist and other group members, they can learn to understand themselves better and develop real alternatives to self-harming behavior.

46. What can parents do about children who harm themselves?

Confronting someone suspected of self-harm can often be an emotionally charged experience, especially for parents dealing with self-harm in one of their children. This also means coming to terms with the underlying issues that might have led to the self-harm in the first place and being willing to take action on their child's behalf.

While parents may blame themselves for missing what would seem like obvious clues in hindsight or wondering if the self-harm stems from something they did wrong, it is more important to show emotional support and get the self-harmer into counseling as soon as possible. Even when self-harmers insist that they have the problem under control, a professional assessment can be essential in identifying why the self-injuring occurred in the first place and how more serious consequences such as suicide may be prevented.

During the treatment process, the role of the parent can be especially critical. Whether by providing support while their child is receiving treatment or even taking part in the treatment directly (e.g., with family counseling), parents need to show their children that they are willing to support them and help them learn more effective ways of coping with emotional problems and stress.

Parents themselves may find that they need counseling to help them work through their own issues and make them better able to cope with what is happening with their children. Support groups allowing parents to share their experiences with other parents of self-harmers can be an important way of coping and can also help them learn more about the kind of problems many self-harmers can face.

Along with being part of the treatment process, parents also need to recognize that the road to recovery isn't always smooth. There are always setbacks, and parents need to recognize this to avoid giving into despair whenever their child suddenly starts to self-harm again unexpectedly. Even if these setbacks occur, it is vital to be as emotionally support-ive as possible and avoid making judgmental statements that can make self-harmers more self-conscious and less likely to be open in future.

Parents also need to be able to follow through in helping their child find closure for whatever issue has been triggering the self-harm in the first place. Whether this involves prior or current abuse of which the par-ent was previously unaware or the child coming to terms with his or her sexual orientation, it is essential that parents be as open and supportive as possible.

This can include being willing to help their child report abuse to the police and seeing them through the often traumatic process of having the abuser go to trial. Since this can take months or years to see through to the end, parents need to be patient and remain supportive at all times.

Unfortunately, many parents often prefer not to believe that abuse has occurred, especially if it involved a close family member or friend. Or else parents might not be willing to accept that their child may be gay or bisexual, another source of trauma that can lead to a vicious cycle of self-harm and shame.

Above all else, parents need to stand by their children, no matter how painful this might be. It is this support that can be most important in helping them to overcome their self-harming and truly move on with their lives.

47. Are there medications that can help with self-harm?

Though there are different types of medications that can be used for treat-ing many of the symptoms often seen in self-harmers, medical doctors need to be extremely cautious in prescribing many of these medications given the potential side effects that can arise. For self-harmers dealing with BPD or obsessive compulsive disorder, for example, atypical anti-psychotics such as aripiprazole (more commonly known as Abilify) and ziprasidone (Geodon or Zeldox) have been shown by researchers to reduce self-harming behavior for up to 18 months after the medication was discontinued.

Interestingly enough, medications that are useful in treating addiction have also shown some benefit in reducing self-harming attempts. For example, naltrexone (also known as Revia or Vivitrol) is an antio-pioid drug that is often prescribed for the treatment of alcoholism and opiate addiction. When used with self-harmers (who are often receiving treatment for substance abuse as well), research has shown that the frequency of self-harm attempts drops significantly compared to baseline. Buprenorphine (marketed as Suboxone and Subutex, among other brand names) is another antiopioid agent that appears to reduce self-harm attempts as well. While other medications, including antidepressants such as venlafaxine (Effexor) and fluoxetine (Prozac), have also been reported to reduce self-harm attempts, the available research data remain limited.

Unfortunately, along with the potential benefits that can occur with medications such as these, there are also potential drawbacks as well given the side effects and health risk associated with the high dosages that are often involved. Along with watching for potential side effects, people taking these medications also need regular blood and urine tests as well as whatever other laboratory tests that the prescribing physician might recommend. Also, medical doctors need to meet with their patients on a regular basis to ensure no problems are developing, including possible interaction effects if more than one type of medication has been prescribed.

Another point to remember is that medication is not a cure-all for the conditions they are meant to treat, especially for problems such as self-harming. This is why many therapists may recommend combined treatment programs that include both group or individual psychotherapy as well as medication to help reduce self-harm attempts and related mental health problems. Since psychotherapists can't prescribe medication in most places, they usually work as a team with the medical doctor who is monitoring the medication that self-harmers may be taking.

At present, there aren't that many research studies looking at the combined effect of medication and counseling in reducing self-harm attempts. The few studies available to date focus on self-harmers who are also diagnosed with personality disorders such as BPD. For these patients, specialized programs combining medication therapy along with group and individual counseling using DBT have produced a sharp drop in self-harm attempts (as much as 50% in one study).

To find the best method for treating self-harmers, physicians may experiment with different medications, especially if there are other mental health problems that are occurring in addition to the self-harming. In all cases, therapists and medical doctors need to monitor patients closely to ensure that no new problems develop.

48. Do online support groups help prevent future self-harm attempts?

As you have already seen in Question 28, there is an active online community for self-harmers, including message boards and support services intended to help people of all ages who are injuring themselves. Some of the more well-established online resources are listed in the Directory of Resources, although Internet resources are subject to change over time. Considering the shame and guilt many self-harmers feel, along with the fact that not every community is going to have treatment programs available, it can be tempting to rely exclusively on these online resources and not bothering with face-to-face treatment with a mental health professional.

Research studies looking at how online services are used show that one-third or more harmers will look online for support in dealing with their self-harm attempts. In general, online help seekers tend to be much more distressed and are also more likely to be suicidal and to injure themselves more severely than self-harmers who don't seek help online. For self-harmers who are in crisis and who feel too isolated and fearful to seek help locally, online services can be a literal lifesaver.

In fact, a substantial minority of self-harmers report in surveys that they prefer to get all the help they need online and avoid face-to-face therapy altogether. Many of these sites can include such resources as peer mentoring with volunteers who have self-harmed themselves and can provide advice and support based on their own experience. Being able to go online to connect with an actual person providing advice in a safe and nonjudgmental way can be a powerful tool for overcoming the resistance to seeking help that self-harmers often experience. Many of these same online resources can also make referrals to local therapists as well.

Online self-harm sites can certainly make self-harmers feel less alone, and the anonymous format can help avoid the sense of guilt and shame that comes with admitting to self-injury and the related emotional issues. Research does suggest that being able to share feelings and personal stories online can help reduce the urge to self-harm and make users feel part of a larger online community.

Despite the powerful support online sites can provide, these resources were never meant to be stand-alone options for people in need. Not all online resources are the same, and some may even be harmful instead. This is especially true of sites that provide graphic content or potentially harmful advice that might make the urge to self-harm even worse.

When looking for help online in dealing with self-harm attempts, users should only deal with sites that are part of established self-help organizations (the sites listed in the Directory of Resources can be a good place to start). While most of these sites are aimed at young people who self-harm, people of all ages can get useful information and advice. Ideally, these sites should only be used as a starting place to get the information needed to make an informed choice about the kind of professional help that they need.

49. Can anything be done about the scars?

For many self-harmers, having to living with the telltale scars that reveal what they have gone through to the world can be traumatic in itself. One alternative that is appealing to many former self-harmers involves covering the scars with artistic tattoos. Tattoo artist Auberon Wolf of British Columbia has made a specialty of this kind of tattoo art, and she has described it as a way to allow her clients to "rewrite" their past traumas and help them move on with their lives.

"You just can't help but think, what can you put there to help the person feel more comfortable in their own skin," said Wolf in a recent interview with CTV News. "What can I bring to that with love and care, that's more than just art?"

Through careful planning that often varies depending on the nature of the scar and the wishes of the client, she is able to create individual designs that can conceal burn marks, scars from self-cutting, mastectomy scars, scars from domestic abuse, and even stretch marks from a traumatic pregnancy.

And Auberon Wolf knows about the importance of life-affirming tattoo work firsthand. A design on her left arm conceals scars stemming from the self-cutting she once engaged in as a teen. Being on-campus during the traumatic Dawson College shooting in 2006 as well as her own experiences with sexual assault has further sensitized her to the link between body scars and trauma. In talking about her own process of recovery, she described her tattooing as an "immense vehicle for personal empowerment."

Her customers certainly agree with this philosophy. As many as 10 clients a week visit Wolf's Vancouver studio and don't seem to mind the long tattooing process, which can take months in some cases. Though not all of them can afford the tattooing, Wolf allows some to pay through barter or traded skills.

A customer who agreed to be part of the interview proudly showed off an elaborate tattoo that hides two scars on her right arm. One of these scars is from a suicide attempt while the other from an intravenous needle used in medical treatment. The tattoo design she chose is a flower bouquet to honor her late mother. Though she reported experiencing flashbacks when the tattooing began, she felt safe and reassured in Wolf's hands. "I now have a beautiful piece of art here," she said while showing off her floral tattoo to reporters. "I'm able to use this as an empowering device. I don't get traumatized anymore."

Not that there is anything unique about Auberon Wolf's work. Tattoo artists worldwide are being recruited to mask scars such as from mastectomies or violence. Some agencies such as Brazil's Municipal Secretariat of Policies for Women are funding female tattoo artists to provide services for trauma survivors.

Still, the tattoo option may not appeal to every self-harmer, and some prefer to leave the scars in place as a way of showing others that self-harming can be overcome. Whatever self-harmers decide to do with their scars, the conscious choice they make represents an important part of the healing process, and many self-harmers may feel the need to discuss what they want to do with therapists, friends, and family before making a decision.

50. Can self-harmers learn to move on with their lives?

As you can see from the examples provided in the Introduction and other sections of this book, there have been many well-known celebrities who have been self-harmers at some point in their lives but who still managed to recover. Whether they succeed in "spinning out" (ending the self-harm attempts) on their own or with the help of therapists and family members, the process can be long and difficult.

Part of the problem in recovering from self-harming is that, much like drug and alcohol abuse, there is the very real risk of "backsliding." Even for self-harmers who manage to go for months, or even years, without any more cuts or burns, new emotional crises or setbacks can strike at any time. Anything that can shake a former self-harmer's confidence can also lead him or her to fall back into old ways of coping, and that includes self-harm attempts. Considering how difficult it can be to quit "cold turkey," it's certainly understandable that many self-harmers are prone to relapses. In online self-harm circles, these relapses are known as "slips" and, not surprisingly, are one of the most common topics discussed.

Though slipping can lead many self-harmers to see themselves as hopeless cases, it is essential not to give in to despair. Setting realistic goals, that is, trying to go without slipping for steadily longer periods of time, can help build up the confidence needed to keep going. Sooner or later, that "last quit" will occur, and the relapses will stop happening.

Even then, moving on to a life after self-harming can be difficult. There are numerous online bulletin boards and websites dedicated to people "in recovery," and many of the people who post there admit that they still think about it once in a while. Though some admit to occasional relapses, being able to talk to others about what they were feeling, whether online or in person, often enable them to work through problems without falling back on old ways of coping.

During this post-self-harm phase, issues such as scar management become more important (see previous question) as well as their attitudes toward these scars. Aside from the tattoo option, some prefer not to hide their scars so they can be reminded of how far they have come and to overcome the sense of shame these scars can bring.

Even for self-harmers who relapse after many years, they may well discover that injuring themselves doesn't have the same benefit it once did. This can be a sign that they have really moved on past the self-harming. Much like thumb-sucking, people may give up self-harming completely once they realize that it had become a part of their past and that better ways of coping are now available.

But there are other risks that self-harmers need to consider. Just because they have moved past the self-harming doesn't necessarily mean they have overcome the emotional issues that led to them harming themselves in the first place. Issues surrounding old traumas, social anxiety, and relationship problems can still resurface, and ex-self-harmers finding that injuring themselves no longer has the same benefits may turn to other ways of coping, including substance abuse or suicide attempts. This is why it is so important that working with a mental health professional needs to continue even after the self-harm attempts have stopped so that patients can develop more positive ways of coping when the inevitable problems develop afterward.

Though the road to recovery is going to be different for every self-harmer, moving on to a life after self-harm attempts requires help from a variety of sources, including therapists, friends, family, and online support from people who have done the same. Despite the occasional relapse, it is essential not to lose hope and to keep trying, no matter what.

❖❖❖

Case Studies

1. STEPHEN

Stephen is a 16-year-old drug and alcohol abuser who has a history of petty offenses and behavior problems. After his latest arrest for breaking and entering, a judge has ordered him to attend anger management and substance abuse counseling. Stephen was also warned that he would be tried as an adult the next time he is arrested. His probation officer has arranged for him to be seen by a clinical psychologist and a social worker to investigate potential treatment programs in the area.

The psychologist interviews Stephen, who had been resisting treatment but is finally agreeing since he doesn't want to risk being sent back to jail or doing time as an adult. On meeting Stephen, she also notes his medical record mentioning the numerous cigarette burns along his arms and legs and that these self-harm episodes go back for years. When he is questioned about these burns, Stephen is reluctant to talk about them at first and simply says that he "doesn't know" why he does it.

While most of the burns were inflicted under the influence of drugs or alcohol, he also admits to hurting himself whenever he is feeling especially stressed. He has even burned himself while in detention (despite his self-harm history, cigarettes are fairly easy to get). In one memorable incident, he carved out several swear words on his right arm, possibly as a way of getting attention and because the sense of pain helped relieve the boredom of being in custody.

When questioned further, Stephen admits that he has been burning himself since the age of 12. This was just about the time of his first arrest as well as when he began using drugs. He denies any history of abuse in his childhood but admits that he grew up in a "rough" neighborhood where gang violence and crack houses were fairly common. While he denies ever using "hard" drugs, he often gets into trouble with the law due to the need to get cash to buy drugs or alcohol.

His mother is a reformed alcoholic, while his father left the family home when Stephen was four years old. Stephen has one half-sister from his mother's later marriage, but his relationship with his stepfather (whom his mother married when he was seven) has always been tense. While there was no physical abuse, Stephen tends to lash out emotionally at his stepfather's attempts at establishing discipline. His half-sister has developmental disabilities requiring special education, and Stephen has often felt jealous of the extra attention she receives.

Though Stephen has participated in several treatment programs in the past (usually aimed at his substance abuse or delinquency), his resolution to stop burning himself rarely lasts long. Being under stress often causes him to revert to burning himself since it is the coping strategy that "works" best for him. His medical file notes ominously that his self-harming attempts are becoming more serious and are starting to require hospital treatment due to the extent of the burns he is inflicting on himself.

His family has expressed concern over the burns, though he has managed to conceal his scars from his friends by wearing loose-fitting clothing with long sleeves. He is somewhat self-conscious about his burns and avoids wearing T-shirts or any other clothes that might let people see the marks along his arms and back.

Through her interviews with Stephen, the psychologist discovers that he is often impulsive and has a history of attention deficit problems, which has led to frequent difficulties in school. Though he denied ever being bullied or getting into fights with other children, Stephen has had a major problem with truancy and was often punished for this by his mother and stepfather.

When younger, he also developed a fascination with fire-setting, though this ended after a fire he set in a trash can near his home got out of control. While he managed to avoid being charged for arson, Stephen never set another fire. Interestingly enough, it was around this time that he began burning himself, though he denies any connection.

On interviewing his mother about Stephen's early medical history, and her own history of alcohol abuse, the mother admits that she had been drinking while pregnant with Stephen, though she cut back on her drinking sharply out of concern for his health. She also notes that Stephen was slightly premature with a low birth weight for which she admits some feeling of guilt due to fear that this was due to her alcohol use.

The psychologist determines that getting through to Stephen requires family counseling as well as one-to-one sessions. Working with his mother and stepfather, she emphasizes that Stephen's impulsiveness means that conventional parenting strategies won't work. For this reason, Stephen's parents are encouraged to avoid nagging at him to behave or threatening him with punishment. If anything, this would produce more stress and increase the likelihood that Stephen would act out, whether through getting high or burning himself. Providing constant positive feedback and encouragement along with establishing concrete rules to follow such as "no drinking" or "tell us when you feel like hurting yourself" are more likely to generate positive results. The psychologist arranges to meet with the parents and probation officer on a regular basis to monitor Stephen's progress and make adjustments as necessary.

Interpretation

Along with Stephen's substance abuse, history of impulsive behavior, and antisocial problems, his history of self-harm attempts makes assessment and treatment more difficult. Given his mother's alcoholism, including her admitting to drinking while pregnant with him, the possibility that Stephen is suffering from the long-term effects of fetal alcohol exposure (FAE) needs to be considered. This is often harder to detect than the full-blown fetal alcohol syndrome (FAS) considering that FAE children lack the telltale signs and medical complications often seen in more severe cases. In Stephen's case, there were early medical signs of potential problems, including premature birth, low birth weight, as well as his later issues with impulsiveness and abiding by rules. His problems with self-harm seem to be linked to his impulsiveness and his difficulty handling stress in positive ways.

Even though the mental and physical issues stemming from FAE can last a lifetime, behavior therapy aimed at curbing impulsive behavior in suspected FAE cases like Stephen can be effective. Working with his mother and stepfather, the psychologist can encourage them to stop focusing on relatively minor slip-ups but instead use rewards to encourage positive behavior, such as spending time with his sister. Providing constant positive feedback and encouragement along with establishing concrete rules to follow such as "no drinking" or "tell us when you feel like hurting yourself" are more likely to generate positive results. It is also important for family members to recognize that patients like Stephen can "fall off the wagon" at any time and have plans in place for when these setbacks occur.

Though behavior therapy aimed at curbing impulsive behavior in suspected FAE cases like Stephen works best for younger children, consistent behavior management can still be useful. This includes changing his environment to make success more likely and monitoring whether or not he is complying with ground rules, which can be difficult for a 17-year-old. Developing a system of rewards for good behavior and steering him toward more positive life choices can help reduce the kind of stress than can lead to self-harm attempts.

2. LAURA

Laura is a 16-year-old child abuse survivor with a history of eating disorders, including several hospital stays. Her periodic binging and purging has developed a disturbing new element since she has recently started cutting herself as well.

The abuse began when Laura was 6 and left alone with a male babysitter who was a friend of the family. Though the babysitter was careful not to leave any physical traces, he did his best to make Laura keep what they were doing hidden from the rest of her family. When Laura was 10, she finally confessed what was happening to her mother who initially didn't believe her. The babysitter had already laid the groundwork to protect himself by talking about Laura's tendency to "tell stories." Although the mother eventually decided to believe Laura and reported the babysitter to Family Services, her initial doubt has had a lingering impact on her relationship with her daughter. Laura also feels guilty over what happened to the babysitter, who was prosecuted, though she never saw him again.

As for the eating disorders, they began when Laura was 14 and she became preoccupied with her appearance. After a friend told her about binging and purging as a way to control weight, Laura started doing the same until the episodes came to damage her health. This led to a new round of confrontation with her mother and sister, her family doctor, and a school counselor, to get Laura to realize how self-destructive her eating disorder was. With encouragement, Laura entered treatment for eating disorders, and her family began to hope that the worst was over since her last hospitalization six months previously, until her sister noticed the scars.

Her sister, Gwen, is five years older than Laura and was a student at the local community college, which meant she didn't spend as much time at home as she did before. Their mother works full-time at a factory on evening shifts, so much of the responsibility for caring for Laura has fallen on Gwen. It was Gwen who realized that the scarring Laura had attributed to "clumsiness" seemed to be occurring more and more often and shared her suspicions with her own friends and the family doctor.

When Gwen confronted Laura over the self-cutting, she initially denied it but became frantic over the possibility that Gwen would tell their mother. After swearing Gwen to secrecy (despite her misgivings), Laura agreed to talk about the self-cutting with her therapist, whom she continues to see on a weekly basis. She also said that the cutting had only started three months earlier after several episodes in which older children tried to bully her.

After inspecting the scars and realizing the full extent of the problem, Gwen decided to tell her mother despite her promise. This angered Laura who accused her sister of betraying her trust and led to tension between them. Since Gwen is also Laura's closest confidante, this has also meant that she is more isolated than ever and less inclined to trust family members with intimate secrets.

Laura's mother tries to be sympathetic, though she directs much of her anger at Gwen whom she accuses of not watching Laura more closely. As a result, Laura feels guiltier than ever and less willing to share any information about the cutting considering the emotion it seems to generate. After phoning Laura's counselor, her mother agrees to meet with her and work out what is to be done next.

During the first joint meeting, the counselor tries to draw out Laura, who is extremely closed off due to her fears about sharing her most intimate thoughts and feelings (especially with her mother present). Laura also admits to deliberately hiding the cutting from her counselor, who had been meeting with her on a regular basis, as well as downplaying her worries about her appearance and the stress she is experiencing in school.

During the course of the meeting, the counselor lays out a treatment plan, which will involve having Laura meeting with her twice a week (as opposed to the once-a-week sessions that they had up to that time). By this point, Laura has worked through her anger at Gwen and agreed not to hide the stress that has led to self-cutting. She is also more open about the lingering effects of her earlier abuse. Through regular sessions and encouraging Laura to be more open with the people in her life, she has learned more positive coping strategies and seems to be handling the stress of school more effectively. While the self-cutting hasn't stopped completely, her counselor is encouraged by Laura's greater openness and her close relationship with her sister.

Interpretation

Research has consistently shown a strong link between different forms of self-harm and childhood sexual abuse (see Question 19). For victims of childhood abuse, posttraumatic symptoms such as flashbacks, intrusive thoughts or images of the trauma, hypervigilance toward anything that might suggest new trauma, and emotional numbing are also frequently experienced and may well account for why self-harming can occur. Two of the most commonly reported reasons many survivors give for self-harm are to control bad feelings and, in many cases, to make themselves feel at all. Using self-cutting or other kinds of self-harm, survivors can cope with unpleasant thoughts and emotions as well as overcome the sense of numbing that often occurs in trauma.

All trauma survivors are prone to episodes during which their symptoms are especially severe. These episodes can occur due to anniversary dates, being in situations that remind them of the trauma, or simply due to the emotional fatigue of dealing with daily life. It is during these episodes that the risk of self-harm is greatest due to the strong need to avoid unpleasant thoughts and simply to break through the sense of numbness that seems so strong at that point.

For child sexual abuse survivors, such as Laura, the need to avoid intrusive memories of abuse can take extreme forms. Along with substance abuse or thoughts of suicide, there is often deep depression and an inability to make emotional contact with the people around them. With many survivors, how severe the injuries they inflict on themselves during their self-harm attempts often depends on how bad the trauma symptoms happen to be at any given time.

Far too many abuse survivors, especially survivors who engage in self-harm attempts, refuse to seek help until being forced into treatment by family members or child care workers. This can mean critical delays in receiving treatment and often allowing self-harm attempts to reach the point of becoming potentially life threatening.

3. ANDREW

Andrew is a 13-year-old young offender who has been sent to a youth reformatory for the first time in his life due to a string of property offenses that he had committed, apparently for the purpose of buying drugs. Admitting to using a wide range of different drugs, primarily cocaine, since the age of 9, Andrew also reported growing up in an abusive home as well as witnessing his father assaulting his mother on numerous occasions.

Emotionally, Andrew tended to be a "powder keg" going off over relatively minor disagreements. This has led to a number of fights in the reformatory and even in the community. His few sexual encounters up to that time had been largely anonymous, and he openly denied any interest in pursuing anything more intimate or long-term. This same loner pattern was seen in his friendships with others his age, and the few friendships he manages to form rarely last long. His inability to form long-term relationships seemed to be tied into his poor self-esteem and general feeling that he is a "loser," with no prospect of a better future.

Though denying any other treatment issues aside from his drug abuse and early history of antisocial behavior, a medical examination turned up something unexpected. Andrew has scars all along his arms as well as his chest and back. When asked about the scarring, Andrew came up with numerous stories about how they came about. First, he insisted that the scars were due to the rough sports he enjoyed playing, and, when it was pointed out to him that the scars didn't really bear that story out, he became agitated and refused to talk about them further.

After Andrew was transferred to the reformatory's treatment wing, the counselor assigned to his case begins meeting him on a regular basis to try drawing him out about his early life and drug abuse. Recognizing that Andrew is sensitive about the scarring, she tries to form a positive therapeutic relationship first to make him more comfortable talking with her about the problems he was facing. She also works with the doctor and nurses who were carefully monitoring Andrew to see if any new scars turn up.

Eventually, Andrew admits that he hurts himself because it is, as he put it, "the only way I can really feel." Dating back to early childhood, the domestic abuse he witnessed, and experienced himself on the few occasions he tried defending his mother, has left him emotionally numbed. The substance abuse began as a way of coping with the internal distress he often felt as he recalled some of the more painful memories from his childhood. He also admits to having an acute fear of being abandoned and is often afraid to form close relationships with anyone, male or female.

He refuses to admit to harming himself because of his general low self-esteem and the sense of shame he has at needing to rely on self-harm as a way to cope. Interestingly enough, several of the young offenders Andrew enjoys hanging out with also show signs of self-harm, though it is hard to determine whether they were copying Andrew or vice versa.

Andrew also admits to thinking about suicide fairly often but denied ever making a serious suicide attempt. During one session with his counselor, he talked about looking at suicide sites online, though he claims this is to read the comments from other suicidal teens, which he regarded as being funny. When questioned about this, he shows significant problems with empathy and being able to understand what other people are feeling. This is something that comes out quite frequently in the way he interacts with other people, and he also has problems in "reading" other people, including facial expressions and body language.

Treating Andrew for his self-harm attempts, along with his substance abuse and other emotional problems, has been extremely difficult. Along with his initial refusal to admit that he was deliberately harming himself, he also has difficulty believing that his self-harm is something he should stop doing. Not only does he see it as an effective way of coping with the stress he faces and to overcome his emotional numbness, but he points out that many of his friends are doing the same thing. He also justifies himself by mentioning some of the self-harm websites he has visited, including community forums where self-harmers meet and discuss ways of self-harming safely. Even though he can be monitored while he is in the reformatory, his therapist fears that he will simply start hurting himself again once he is released. While he is cooperating with his therapist for now, getting Andrew to stay in treatment is likely to be an uphill battle.

Interpretation

Though never formally diagnosed, Andrew is already showing many signs of borderline personality disorder (BPD), including his history of unstable relationships, impulsive behavior, fear of abandonment, problems regulating his emotions, poor self-esteem, and inability to recognize internal mental states. With people showing BPD symptoms, self-harm attempts can be extremely common, especially as a strategy for coping with stress. For this reason, the latest version of the *Diagnostic and Statistical Manual of Mental Disorder* lists self-harm as one of the main symptoms, which can be used to diagnose BPD. Though they are often found together, BPD and self-harm are definitely separate conditions, with research showing less than half of all people who self-harm meeting criteria for a BPD diagnosis.

Therapists providing treatment for self-harming adolescents with BPD symptoms need to advise their patients about the risks associated with being around other young people who might also be harming themselves. The risk of a "contagion effect" is especially high for adolescents who are receiving inpatient treatment, whether in a hospital or a reformatory, which is why ground rules need to be laid down to reduce the risk of influencing other patients to harm themselves.

For patients who self-harm and who also have BPD symptoms, however, the prognosis is often poor because of the difficulty with treating both conditions at the same time. There are several different forms of long-term psychotherapy that can be effective in treating BPD, though it often depends on how willing patients are to change. Though the symptoms may not disappear completely, treatment can help patients like Andrew learn better ways to cope with emotional distress and function more effectively in the long run.

4. RICK

While Rick tends not to admit to having a problem with alcohol, his family and friends think differently. Now 27 years old, his history of drinking goes back to young adulthood and the frequent benders he went on with his college friends throughout his university years. Even after graduating, the benders continued on a semiregular basis, though he is usually able to hold it together long enough not to get fired from the various jobs he has held over the years.

Not that there haven't been problems, however. An impaired driving charge three years earlier cost him a job as a courier, and it took him years to get his license back. After a recent incident at a company social function, Rick had to complete a mandatory alcohol counseling program. Perhaps more alarmingly, a recent medical examination has turned up early signs of liver damage, and his doctor has been urging him to quit drinking completely.

Whether due to the stress of coping with his drinking or the pressure he is getting from his parents, his medical doctor, who has been seeing him monthly to monitor his progress, is noticing that Rick has several marks that appear to be due to cigarette burns. Even though Rick dismissed the first marks the doctor found as being due to an accident that occurred during a bender, the marks seem to be part of a regular pattern that is occurring more frequently. When questioned about the marks, Rick admits that he has been burning himself during his benders but he isn't certain why.

After learning about the scars and his recent history of burning (which Rick had never told them about), his parents made arrangements for him to see a psychologist. Though Rick insists that he didn't need any more counseling, he finally agrees to go. During the first meeting, Rick admits to the psychologist that he has been burning himself but emphatically denied ever harming himself when he wasn't drinking. He also insists that he would be able to stop burning himself once he gets his drinking under control (a promise he had made to his parents before but has never been able to keep).

During this interview, Rick also admits that he attempted suicide when he was 18. While he put that attempt down to being "stupid" and being heavily influenced by the suicide of a close friend, Rick does tend to act impulsively, something that has gotten him into trouble in the past. He also has a history of short-term romantic relationships and has never been involved with anyone longer than six months. Though Rick denies that his drinking played a role in his frequent breakups, at least one friend admitted that it has, more than once.

His drinking has also cost him some long-term friendships. Though he continues to hang out with a regular clique of people he enjoys socializing with, the fact that they happen to be "drinking buddies" who enable his drinking is contributing to the problem.

During treatment for his drinking, Rick opens up about some of his experiences in college and the emotional problems that drove his alcoholism. He also describes the sexual abuse he experienced in early high school from a fellow student who had been bullying him. Though it only occurred several times before the bully's interest moved on to other students, Rick continues to experience discomfort as he recalls what happened to him. Since he never admitted to the abuse before (and the bully was never charged), Rick was left to cope with the memories and his own emotional turmoil over his sexual identity on his own.

In college, many of the people he went drinking with often made jokes about homosexuality, which caused him to reexperience the trauma he is suppressing. He considers alcohol to be an effective way of controlling the anxiety he often experiences, especially whenever he feels stressed due to problems at work or in social situations.

Though he is uncertain why he started hurting himself, he admits that the alcohol is not as effective as it used to be and he is feeling more isolated and anxious than ever. He also admits that not all of the self-burning had taken place when he had been drinking. On one or two occasions, he discovered new burns, though he had no memory of injuring himself. What disturbed him more was that he knew that alcohol couldn't have been involved since he was sober when the burns occurred. This is what spurred him to seek treatment.

Interpretation

While self-harm is most often thought of as occurring in young people, it can begin at virtually any age. And, while it is most common in women, the number of reported cases of self-harm in men has been slowly rising in recent years. If anything, self-harm can be more serious when it occurs in men since they are less likely to seek medical help and are often more likely to inflict severe injuries on themselves.

Part of the problem rests with gender roles, with men being expected to "tough out" injuries and to downplay the kind of psychological problems that might lead them to self-harm. Some men even go so far as to claim they were trying to commit suicide because they were too embarrassed to admit they were using self-harm to cope. When it comes to the trauma that often accompanies sexual abuse, men are also far less likely to admit to having been victimized. This means that they are far less likely than women to seek out help and often rely on inappropriate ways of coping to deal with the emotional distress that memories of abuse can bring out.

In Rick's case, it's important to note that self-harm can occur both directly and indirectly. Indirect self-harm can take the form of substance abuse (e.g., as his drinking) and high-risk behaviors (e.g., reckless driving or unsafe sex). Other examples of indirect self-harm that are linked to typically male stereotypes of behavior include smashing beer cans on their foreheads, punching walls, "picking fights," and betting or daring friends to engage in high-risk activities with a strong possibility of harm. But when the indirect methods of coping begin to fail and the emotional distress becomes strong enough, direct self-harm can develop.

Since this kind of self-harm tends to be impulsive (and most likely to occur under the influence of drugs or alcohol), self-harming men might not want to acknowledge what is happening. For Rick, and others like him, treatment usually focuses on getting them to be honest with themselves about the emotions that are feeding into their substance abuse and self-harm. With time and determination though, progress can be made.

5. CLAIRE

Claire, a 19-year-old high school student, has a history of anxiety attacks and self-cutting episodes that has left numerous scars along both her arms. The self-cutting began when she was 14 and already dealing with anorexia. Being self-conscious about her weight added to the stress she was experiencing dealing with unkind remarks she was getting from other students in her school. While her parents were sympathetic, they often left her on her own during the day since they both worked long hours. Her older sister had already left for college, and Claire felt more isolated than ever. That was when the cutting began, though it rarely progressed to the point of needing medical treatment. Once or twice, when the cutting was severe enough to need stitches, Claire passed it off as being due to her "clumsiness" in accidentally cutting herself on broken glass, though she was careful not to attract too much attention by cutting herself so deeply again.

It was only when her family doctor found the scars following a medical exam (which she had managed to avoid for months) that Claire was forced into treatment. Her mother was particularly upset that something like this was happening without her noticing, though Claire had been very good at concealing the self-cutting from everyone she knew. Several of her friends later admitted knowing as well, though they had been afraid to tell anyone since Claire made them promise to keep her secret. She also compensated by being extra cheerful in social situations since she didn't want anyone to think she was potentially suicidal.

Claire admitted to visiting several online sites catering to self-cutters and even two suicide sites to get information on suicide methods. While she did consider suicide and even made an active plan at one point, she changed her mind because she didn't want to hurt her family. Ironically, the emotional stress of deciding not to commit suicide led to a particularly bad wrist-cutting episode, though she managed to conceal it from everybody.

After participating in several treatment programs, including a group program for self-harmers that had recently started up in her community, Claire eventually ended the self-harm episodes. While she continues to have lingering health problems stemming from her anorexia, which she also got under control, Claire has developed better ways of handling stress.

But the very visible scarring along both her arms and legs continues to make her feel self-conscious. Though her family and friends now know about the self-cutting and have provided their full acceptance of what she went through, she hates having to share these details with people she is meeting for the first time. Not only is she reluctant to share her mental health history with other people her own age, but she also worries about her appearance. She conceals the scars with long sleeves to cover her arms and avoids wearing anything revealing like swimsuits or shorts. Her fears about her appearance are also affecting how she approaches new romantic relationships since she is uncertain about when she should begin sharing details with any new love interest of what was a very dark period in her early life.

"What am I supposed to say to someone I really like?" she asks. "Am I supposed to admit I was such a weirdo when I was younger? Is it anyone's business what I did so long ago?"

While Claire continues to attend counseling with a therapist who has experience dealing with self-harm cases, this is still an uphill battle for her because she is self-conscious about her appearance. Though she has gone on occasional dates, Claire tends to put emotional barriers between herself and any potential love interest due to her own internal qualms about sharing personal details of her life.

She has recently started seeing a man her age, Don, who seems interested in her and already knows about her self-harm history since they grew up in the same neighborhood. Though he assures her that she looks fine, Claire continues to resist wearing anything that might reveal her scars for fear that total strangers might judge her.

Don tries to be sympathetic, though Claire's reluctance to take their relationship to the next level and become intimate has put a strain on things. Though he tries not to pressure her and has already spoken to her therapist about his concerns, Claire is convinced that he is planning to break up with her soon. Since so much of her own self-esteem is tied up in her worries about her appearance, she views the prospect of a breakup as a major calamity in her life.

Interpretation

Even after the self-harming stops, the physical reminders, including visible scars along the arms and legs, thighs, and stomach, can be extremely difficult to explain away or hide. For many people, having a history of self-harm is often seen as being shameful or embarrassing. As a result, it is hardly surprising that people with visible scars often prefer to avoid awkward questions by concealing them any way they can. This reluctance to open up about the past can lead many former self-harmers to isolate themselves from others, including refusing to become physically intimate.

While there are creative solutions for concealing scars, including artistic tattooing (see Question 49), the real issue is the need to come to terms with the emotions linked to the scars themselves. Keeping scars hidden is one way many survivors rely on to suppress painful memories as well as their own fears that the self-harming might start up again. Through supportive counseling, former self-harmers can learn to become more comfortable discussing their history and also to recognize that overcoming past adversity such as self-harm is nothing to be guilty or ashamed about.

By learning how to focus on their own feelings and opening up about their reasons for sharing details about an extremely dark time in their lives, self-harmers can overcome their own sense of isolation and become more comfortable sharing intimate information with other people in their lives. For Claire, and many others like her, learning how to talk about the scars, including being willing to educate people about nonsuicidal self-injury and how common it really is, remains the best way for former self-harmers to move on with their lives.

Glossary

Alexithymia: A personality trait characterized by inability to identify feelings or emotions as well as being unable to recognize emotions in others. People high in alexithymia often have extreme difficulty forming social attachments or appreciating how other people are feeling. While not considered a mental health disorder in itself, alexithymia is often confused with borderline and antisocial personality disorder, though they are very different. It can be a significant predictor of self-harming behavior.

Automatic negative reinforcement behavior: Self-harming behavior used as a way of escaping from negative emotions or relieving tension. It's a part of the four-function model of self-harm proposed by Matthew Nock and Mitchell Prinstein.

Automatic positive reinforcement behavior: Self-harming behavior intended to produce a positive emotional or mental state. It can include the emotional "high" some self-harmers report following a self-harm attempt. It's a part of the four-function model of self-harm proposed by Matthew Nock and Mitchell Prinstein.

Automatic thoughts: Beliefs that shape what patients think about themselves, the people around them, and the world in general. These automatic thoughts are often formed by traumatic early life experiences that can create a distorted view of the world and themselves. For self-harmers, these automatic thoughts can include such beliefs as "I deserve to be punished," "Nobody cares about me," "I am worthless," or "Cutting myself is the only way to take away the pain." Cognitive restructuring can be effective in overcoming automatic thoughts.

Avoidant personality disorder (APD): A chronic pattern of impaired personality functioning, also known as anxious personality disorder. This diagnosis is often given to people reporting strong feelings of inadequacy, social anxiety, a fear of being judged by others, and avoidance of social interaction despite wanting to be close to others.

Borderline personality disorder (BPD): A chronic pattern of impaired personality functioning usually identified by problems with mood instability, erratic behavior, impaired self-image, and poor social functioning. Often occurring with other mental health problems such as anger, depression, or anxiety, people suffering from BPD are often prone to self-harm along with other concerns such as substance abuse and suicidal thinking. Usually identified in early adulthood, BPD often begins in early childhood and can be linked to childhood abuse or trauma as well as issues with parental neglect. Treatment programs such as cognitive behavior therapy have been effective in helping BPD patients recover.

Cognitive behavioral therapy (CBT): A form of psychotherapy that has proven to be highly effective in treating a range of problems, including self-harm behavior and personality disorders. Through group or individual treatment sessions, patients can learn to change their underlying core beliefs about themselves and the people around them. As a result, CBT can reduce the emotional and behavioral problems often associated with personality disorders, self-harm, and suicidal thinking.

Cognitive distortions: Ways that our minds convince us of something that isn't true and that reinforce the negative beliefs associated with depression and other mood problems. Examples of cognitive distortions include filtering (focusing entirely on negative aspects of a situation while ignoring the positive ones), catastrophizing (always believing the worst-case scenario will happen), all-or-none thinking (seeing things in black and white without recognizing that there is a middle ground), or overgeneralization (making broad conclusions based on very limited experience).

Cognitive restructuring: The therapeutic process of helping patients recognize and change the cognitive distortions that lead to *automatic thoughts* and learning to overcome these distortions and change their beliefs. During the treatment process, patients learn to challenge these beliefs and identify the cognitive errors they have made. There are a wide range of different possible techniques that can be explored during treatment sessions, and therapists may select the ones that may be most effective for each patient.

Decentering: A mindfulness training technique that involves learning to stop reacting to thoughts and feelings that might trigger negative emotions or beliefs and simply accepting them without judgment.

Decoupling: A technique similar to decentering that involves reducing or eliminating the link between inner experiences (e.g., depression or anxiety) and external behaviors (e.g., self-harming).

Dialectical behavior therapy (DBT): Focusing on mindfulness, or basic awareness of one's own emotions and how they can affect behavior, dialectical behavior therapy can be used to help patients learn to control self-destructive behavior and improve social relationships. DBT also deals with the dialectical tension between a patient's need for acceptance and the need for change. It can be used individually or in group sessions and has become extremely popular in treating self-harmers and people with personality disorders around the world.

Dissociation: A sense of detachment from reality that often occurs as a symptom of posttraumatic stress. Occurring on a continuum, dissociation can range from mild symptoms such as daydreaming while driving a car to more severe forms such as traumatic amnesia or dissociative identity disorder. Other forms of dissociation can include the sense that the world isn't real, psychological numbing, and apathy or lack of interest in outside interests. Many self-harmers report injuring themselves as a way of breaking through the dissociation they are experiencing and to make themselves "feel" again.

Dynamic deconstructive psychotherapy: Known as DDP for short, this is a psychodynamic therapy designed to help self-harmers come to terms with their emotions and improve relationships. Primarily aimed at patients with borderline personality disorder, early research suggests that it can be effective for self-harmers as well.

Eating disorders: Serious disturbances in eating behavior such as extreme and unhealthy refusal to eat or overeating, often due to emotional distress or obsessive thoughts about physical appearance or body weight. The most common eating disorders are anorexia nervosa (refusing to eat), bulimia nervosa (extreme overeating followed by purging), and binge eating disorder (eating to deal with distress). Believed to affect about 25 million Americans alone (75% of whom are female), eating disorders are also linked to mental health issues such as depression, social anxiety, and early childhood trauma.

Emo: A rock music genre that has become the center of an underground subculture. Emo fans are often identifiable by listening to music by emo bands such as Death Cab for Cutie, clothing styles such as wearing black wristbands, characteristic hair styles, and an outward display of gloominess and depression, complete with self-harm behavior and body piercing. Emo music has also been implicated in the suicides of some fans, and critics suggest that its "glamorizing" of death has led to an increase in suicidal behavior and self-harming, though fans dispute this. It's often confused with goth culture despite some similarities.

Emotion regulated group therapy: Also referred to as ERGT, this is a specialized form of dialectical behavior therapy specifically designed for treating borderline personality disorder and self-harming. Usually administered in a 14-week group format, ERGT focuses on developing emotional regulation skills and acceptance as well as how to pursue important goals. While not as widely researched as DBT, studies have shown significant reduction in self-harming behavior over a nine-month period following the end of treatment.

Excoriation disorder: Also known as skin-picking disorder or dermatillomania, excoriation disorder involves the repeated urge to pick at one's own skin, often to the point of causing damage. While usually classified as a form of obsessive-compulsive disorder, it often resembles substance abuse in many ways. Cases of suspected excoriation disorder should be referred to a qualified medical professional right away so that proper treatment can begin.

Fetal alcohol exposure/Fetal alcohol effect: Mental and physical issues stemming from exposure to alcohol during pregnancy. Though fetal alcohol effect is much subtler than the full-blown fetal alcohol effect syndrome, children can still develop problems with low birth weight and later issues with impulsivity and poor coping strategies such as self-harm.

Gateway theory: A theory suggesting that self-harm attempts can serve as a gateway to later suicide or suicide attempts as the self-harming behavior escalates.

Grounding: The process of becoming more detached from emotional pain and become more centered and focused. Grounding techniques can include plunging the hands into very cold water or rubbing ice cubes on the skin to provide some relief from the tension of wanting to self-harm. Other techniques can include twanging a rubber band on the skin, eating hot peppers, or sniffing a nasal decongestant.

Harm avoidance: A personality trait or behavior pattern characterized by excessive worrying, social anxiety, self-doubt, fatigue, pessimism, and fear of uncertainty. Along with being linked to early childhood problems such as trauma or abuse, brain research has also associated harm avoidance with reduced gray matter in key regions of the brain. Studies show that people reporting self-harm along with other problems such as an eating disorder often tend to be high in harm avoidance.

High-betrayal sexual abuse: Sexual abuse involving a trusted adult such as a parent, close family member, or caregiver. It can be especially traumatic for children given the sense of betrayal stemming from the actions of a supposedly trusted adult. Along with this violation of trust, abuse victims are often into concealing their abuse out of fear that they wouldn't be believed or would be blamed for encouraging the abuse in the first place.

Impulsivity: A personality trait or behavior of a multifactorial construct that involves a tendency to act on a whim, displaying behavior characterized by little or no forethought, reflection, or consideration of the consequences. According to one prominent model, there are different kinds of impulsivity, including mood-based impulsivity (rash or impulsive behavior in response to negative emotions such as sadness or anxiety), sensation seeking (a preference for new or risky experiences), lack of perseverance (abandoning attempts to reach goals), and lack of premeditation (acting rashly without considering the consequences). Research suggests that problems controlling impulses is a common problem with self-harmers.

Indirect self-harm behavior: Engaging in activities that have a reasonable risk of experiencing bodily harm even when there isn't a conscious intention of self-harm. These are often justified as "thrill-seeking" activities, including bizarre "bonding" practices such as smashing beer cans with a forehead, shooting staples into legs, punching walls or each other, and even engaging in "dares" or stunts to prove courage. It can also include "hazing" rituals to gain acceptance into a social group.

Internalized homophobia: The self-loathing that many sexual minority individuals experience when they internalize the harmful messages they hear about being homosexual or transgender. Believing that they are inferior or damaged because they aren't part of the heterosexual majority can lead to emotional distress and a need to punish themselves, whether through self-harming or suicide attempts.

Lesch-Nyhan syndrome (LNS): A rare inherited disorder caused by a deficiency of key enzymes and the buildup of uric acid in body tissues. Symptoms can include bizarre self-mutilating behavior beginning as early as the second year of life as well as neurological indicators such as facial grimacing, repetitive movements of the arms and legs, and involuntary writhing. Diagnosis is often difficult in the early stages since behavioral symptoms can often be confused with other conditions. Prognosis is poor in severe cases, though milder cases can be successfully treated.

Manchester self-harm rule (MASH): A set procedure developed by health care professionals in Manchester, United Kingdom, for identifying high-risk self-harmers. Under this rule, patients are classified as high-risk for repeated self-harm or suicide if they have a previous history of suicide or self-harm attempts, have a history of psychiatric treatment, are receiving current psychiatric treatment, and have a history of benzodiazepine use. While mostly intended to deal with high-risk cases, the MASH rule can help identify self-harmers and allow hospitals to act more effectively in finding them effective mental health care.

Manual assisted cognitive therapy: Known as MACT for short, this is a six-session focused therapy program designed to help patients understand why they are harming themselves, to relieve distress, and find more constructive ways of coping with their problems. Sessions follow a manual-based approach with units such as "Understanding Self-Harm" and "What to Do in a Crisis." Along with individual therapy, patients rely on bibliotherapy to learn more about self-harming and coping. MACT shows promise in reducing self-harm attempts and may be preferable to other approaches since it can be completed in a relatively short time period.

Mindfulness: A mental state focusing on the present moment instead of the past or future. This kind of awareness can be attained through mental training and techniques such as meditation and deep breathing exercises. Originally part of Buddhist and Hindu philosophies, mindfulness has become an important concept in Western medicine in recent years. Mindfulness training has become a valuable component in the treatment of a wide range of physical and psychiatric conditions, including depression, stress management, substance abuse, and, more recently, self-harming.

Mindfulness-based relapse prevention: Known as MBRP for short, this is a form of therapy proven effective in treating substance abuse as well as compulsive behaviors such as gambling and self-harm. Research shows a significant drop in self-harm attempts as compared to nontreated self-harmers, though such research is still in the very early stages.

Nonsuicidal self-injury (NSSI): The act of deliberately injuring yourself without the intention of committing suicide. While the most common form of NSSI is self-cutting, it can also involving burning, scratching, head-banging, consuming harmful substances, and so forth as well as deliberately preventing injuries from healing. Tattoos and body piercing are usually not considered to be examples of NSSI unless they were carried out with the intention of inflicting bodily harm. NSSI is most commonly carried out on the wrists, hands, stomach, legs, or thighs but can occur on any part of the body.

Onychophagia: Compulsive nail biting. Most common in children, onychophagia is classified as an impulsive control disorder if the symptoms become too severe. Health problems associated with chronic nail biting include bacterial and viral infections as well as mouth lesions and deformed fingernails. It can be treated successfully with behavior therapy.

Painful and provocative experiences (PPE): Traumatic life experiences that lead to individuals overcoming their fear of pain and acquiring a reduced sense of self-preservation leading to a greater capability for self-harm or suicide. These can include early childhood physical, emotional, or sexual abuse, severe trauma, or exposure to domestic violence. These are an important part of Thomas Joiner's interpersonal theory of suicide.

Patient safety improvement (PSI) program: This is a program established by the Veterans Administration (VA) to identify ways of preventing suicide in returning veterans receiving care. While focusing primarily on suicide, different types of self-injury are also targeted whether suicide was intended or not. Veterans who injure themselves are substantially more likely to be diagnosed with depression or other emotional disorders, substance abuse, and PTSD. Among self-injuries, 32 percent also had a diagnosis of personality disorder. With treatment provided through PSI and similar programs, veterans can learn to cope with stress and find effective alternative to self-harming behavior.

Perceived burdensomeness: The belief that one has become a burden to friends and family and that they will be better off after he or she dies. It's a belief that is commonly found in self-harmers and people attempting suicide.

Perseverance: The ability to persist in a certain goal or purpose despite difficulties or obstacles. People who are highly impulsive often have difficulty with perseverance making them more easily frustrated. Research looking at self-harmers suggests that they may often have a problem with perseverance, among other personality issues.

Physical addiction: This refers to the body forming a physiological dependence on a given substance such as alcohol or narcotics, often to the point of developing severe withdrawal effects if someone tries to quit "cold turkey." It's not to be confused with psychological dependence.

Posttraumatic stress disorder: Also known as PTSD, posttraumatic stress disorder is defined as a condition of persistent mental and emotional stress occurring as a result of injury or severe psychological shock such as exposure to a life-threatening or emotionally damaging event. Symptoms can include disturbed sleep, flashback, intrusive memories, as well as dissociation. It can often be seen in cases of self-harming behavior.

Psychological dependence: For addicts, it is also possible to form a psychological dependence with the addictive substance or even specific behaviors such as gambling, which causes it to become an essential part of someone's ability to cope with stress or emotional problems.

Safety contract: An agreement formed by therapists and patients in the early stages of treatment for self-harm behavior. Much like no-suicide contract, self-harm contracts basically lay down ground rules for self-harm. It's often used to minimize the health risks for self-harming and to encourage patients to be open and aware of their underlying triggers as well as trying to find more constructive ways of dealing with stress or frustration.

Schema-focused therapy: A form of psychotherapy that combines cognitive behavioral therapy with other forms of psychotherapy to help people with self-harm and personality disorder symptoms overcome the poor self-image that often lies at the root of their problems. By learning to think better about themselves, patients can learn how to interact with people around them in a more positive way and develop more positive social skills.

Self-harm diary: A record of self-harm attempts written by patients as part of the treatment process. Along with recording the attempts, patients writing these diaries also describe what led up to the self-harming, including emotional state, situational pressures, and daily problems. These diaries can be helpful in identifying triggers and in learning to diffuse the emotions that can lead to self-harming.

Self-medication: As proposed by psychiatrists Edward Khantzian and Mark Albanese, *self-medication* involves the use of drugs or alcohol as a way of relieving or changing painful mental states. Whether due to early trauma, poor self-esteem, relationship problems, or as a way of coping with unhappiness, different addictive substances can have different effects, and users may often experiment before finding something that "works" for them.

Slips: Self-harm community slang term for relapses.

Social alienation: A sense of being isolated or not belonging to something larger, whether it is a family, a circle of friends, or some other social group that is considered valuable.

Social cognitive theory: A theory of human social behavior first proposed by psychologist Albert Bandura. According to this theory, people of all ages can learn new behaviors by observing other people modeling this behavior. This modeling effect can also make people more likely to engage in behaviors they have already learned. Along with models they may interact with in person, repeated exposure to movies or television featuring people engaging in certain kinds of behavior can increase the likelihood of people copying this behavior, especially if they identify strongly with the characters they are seeing. This can account for the copycat effect that often makes people more likely to engage in harmful behaviors such as cigarette smoking, violent behavior, suicide, and self-harming behavior.

Social contagion: A form of social influence in which a certain behavior or emotional state can spread from one member of a group to other group members through simple imitation or even exposure to media stories describing the behavior. This can apply to the spread of popular "memes," including new hairstyles, new fashions in clothing, and patterns of speech, and can also apply to drug and alcohol abuse, unsafe sex, or other forms of dangerous behavior that can become widely copied because the "cool kids" are doing it. It can also account for copycat suicides as well as self-harm behavior occurring following a news story about a celebrity doing something similar.

Social negative reinforcement behavior: Self-harming behavior used to escape a toxic situation or avoid confrontation with somebody else. It's a part of the four-function model of self-harm proposed by Matthew Nock and Mitchell Prinstein.

Social positive reinforcement behavior: Self-harming behavior intended to show others that they need help or that their problems need to be taken seriously. It can be confused with "attention seeking." It's a part of the four-function model of self-harm proposed by Matthew Nock and Mitchell Prinstein.

Spinning out: Self-harm community slang term for ending self-harming behavior.

Sublimation: A coping strategy that involves replacing destructive behaviors (e.g., self-harming) with more positive activities. For example, instead of punching a wall, self-harmers can be taught to punch a pillow or beat a drum. Other activities that can keep the hands busy include writing, drawing, sculpting with clay or Plasticine, crocheting, or ripping paper.

Transference focused psychotherapy: Known as TFP for short, this is a psychodynamic therapy designed to help self-harmers come to terms with their emotions and improve relationships. Primarily aimed at patients with borderline personality disorder, early research suggests that TFP can be effective for self-harmers as well.

Trichotillomania: Compulsive hair-pulling behavior. It's classified as an impulse control disorder, which is often associated with obsessive-compulsive disorder. Much like self-harming, hair-pulling episodes can be triggered by anxiety, and many people with trichotillomania may not be aware that that they are pulling their hair. Often running in families, trichotillomania may have a genetic component, though it can be successfully treated with CBT and medication.

Urban primitive movement: A new trend in body modification linked to a 1989 book, *Modern Primitives*, by Roland Loomis, a.k.a. Fakir Musafar. Advocates of the urban primitive movement often engage in body modification such as scarification, flesh hook suspending, corset training, body piercing, branding, and tattooing adapted from "primitive" traditional societies. Often intended as a "rite of passage," many engage in this kind of body modification due to spiritual curiosity or as a form of personal growth.

Voice-movement therapy: Originally developed by therapist Paul Newham, voice-movement therapy (VMT for short) is a form of expressive arts therapy using singing, drama, expressive writing, sound-making, massage, and movement activities to help patients regulate their emotions and increase self-awareness. While only a few studies have been completed to date, VMT shows early promise in treating self-harmers.

Wrist-cutting syndrome: An early term used to describe self-harming behavior, primarily in women. It was later discarded as the true scope of self-harming became identified.

Directory of Resources

While most cities have local resources that can be found through your family doctor or mental health organizations, here is a list of online resources that can be accessed for more information.

WEBSITES AND NATIONAL ORGANIZATIONS

Self-Injury Outreach and Services (SIOS). Part of a collaboration between McGill University in Montreal and the University of Guelph, SIOS runs a website providing resources for self-harmers, self-harm survivors, and their family members. The website lists personal stories about self-harm as well as information sheets and an up-to-date resource section. http://sioutreach.org/

Recover Your Life. One of the most well-known online communities for self-harmers, Recover Your Life offers online forums and a chat line run by volunteers allowing immediate help for everyone in need. The website also provides articles and general information as well as assistance finding local resources. http://www.recoveryourlife.com/

Self-Injury and Recovery Research and Resources (SIRRR). Operated by Cornell University's College of Human Ecology, the Cornell Research Program on Self-Injury and Recovery provides a website summarizing its research as well as providing information on self-harm, including resources for self-harmers, schools, parents, and health care professionals. http://www.selfinjury.bctr.cornell.edu/

To Write Love on Her Arms (TWLOHRA). Founded in 2007 and taking its name from a short story written by its founder, this nonprofit organization seeks to share stories about self-harm survivors and promote greater understanding about why people harm themselves. They also operate a website and a blog as well as conduct events across the United States to raise awareness about self-harm. https://twloha.com/

SAFE Alternatives. Standing for Self Abuse Finally Ends, the SAFE Foundation was founded in 1986 to provide treatment for self-harmers. Its website also provides a national network for treatment professionals as well as educational resources for self-harmers, friends, and family. http://www.selfinjury.com/

Self-Injury Foundation. A Michigan-based organization providing educational and treatment information surrounding self-injury. Its website provides therapist referrals and educational materials for anyone in need as well as an updated list of hotline numbers across the United States and in many other countries as well. The foundation also conducts year-round media events promoting awareness, including Self-Injury Awareness Day every March 1. http://www.selfinjuryfoundation.org/index.html

International Society for the Study of Self-injury (ISSS). Founded in 2006, the ISSS is an international coalition of researchers, health care professionals, and students with an interest in understanding, assessing, and treating nonsuicidal self-injury. Along with conducting annual conferences to promote self-harm research, ISSS also provides a professional network allowing international collaboration on research and treatment initiatives. http://itriples.org/redesadmin15/

While not dealing with self-injury specifically, these other organizations should be mentioned too:

CHADSCoalition. Founded after Marian and Larry McCord's 18-year-old son, Chad, died by suicide in 2004, the Communities Healing Adolescent Depression and Suicide Coalition offers school outreach programs, community awareness presentations and classes, as well as family support programs to advance the awareness and prevention of depression and suicide. Providing a network of volunteers and student ambassadors to help vulnerable teens, the coalition also provides specialized school programs, including SOS Signs of Suicide and the Olweus Bullying Prevention programs. http://www.chadscoalition.org/

National Alliance on Mental Illness (NAMI). The largest grassroots organization in the United States dedicated to helping people overcome problems with mental illness. NAMI has local branches in most major cities as well as provides a website listing essential resources on a wide range of topics, including depression and self-harm. NAMI also provides a national helpline and special services for teens and young adults, veterans, and sexual minority members who are seeking help in their own communities. http://nami.org/

BOOKS

Self-Harm

Adler, P., & Adler, P. (2011). *The tender cut: Inside the hidden world of self-injury.* New York: New York University Press.

Schmide, U., & Davidson, K. (2004). *Life after self-harm: A guide to the future.* New York: Brunner-Routledge.

Walsh, B.W. (2012). *Treating self-injury: A practical guide.* New York: Guildford Press.

TRAUMA AND ABUSE

Bain, O., & Saunders, M. (1990). *Out in the open: A guide for young people who have been sexually abused.* London, England: Virago.

Kennerly, H. (2000). *Overcoming childhood trauma.* London, England: Robinson.

Relationship Issues

Amodeo, J., & Wentworth, K. (1986). *A guide to successful relationships.* London, England: Arkana.

Skynner, R., & Cleese, J. (1983). *Families and how to survive them.* London, England: Methuen.

ONLINE ARTICLES

Hendricksen, E. Self-injury: 4 reasons people cut and what to do. Retrieved from https://www.psychologytoday.com/blog/how-be-yourself/201610/self-injury-4-reasons-people-cut-and-what-do

Hicks, J. Help! My child is injuring himself. Retrieved from https://www.psychologytoday.com/blog/raising-parents/201612/help-my-child-is-injuring-himself

Muller, R. T. Self-harm: Know the signs, help a friend. Retrieved from https://www.psychologytoday.com/blog/talking-about-trauma/201406/self-harm-know-the-signs-help-friend

Smith, M. Cutting and self-harm: How to feel better without hurting yourself. Retrieved from https://www.helpguide.org/articles/anxiety/cutting-and-self-harm.htm

Index

About the Author

Romeo Vitelli, PhD, C.Psych, is a clinical psychologist in private practice in Toronto and Hamilton, Ontario. Prior to going into private practice, he was a staff psychologist at Millbrook Correctional Centre, a maximum-security prison in eastern Ontario, and also ran the Sex Offender Treatment Program in Hamilton, Ontario, for a number of years. He received his bachelor's degree from the University of Windsor and his master's and doctoral degrees from York University in Toronto, Canada. His current practice focuses on clinical neuropsychology, forensic psychology, and pain management, and he has treated a wide variety of disorders, including posttraumatic stress disorder, substance abuse, depression, chronic pain, and personality disorders in inpatient and outpatient settings. In addition to his book, *The Everything Guide for Overcoming PTSD*, which came out in 2014, he is an active blogger and regular contributor to *Psychology Today* and the *Huffington Post*.